MODERN MACHINE QUILTING

MAKE A PERFECTLY
FINISHED QUILT
ON YOUR
HOME MACHINE

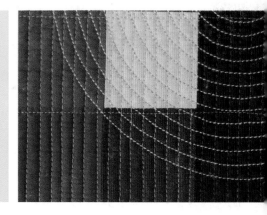

Catherine Redford

Fons&Porter

Published by Fons & Porter Books, an imprint of F+W Media, Inc., 10151 Carver Road, Suite 200, Blue Ash, Ohio 45242. (800) 289-0963. First Edition.

a content + ecommerce company

www.fwcommunity.com

21 20 19 18 17   5 4 3 2 1

Distributed in Canada by Fraser Direct
100 Armstrong Avenue
Georgetown, ON, Canada L7G 5S4
Tel: (905) 877-4411

Distributed in the U.K. and Europe by F&W MEDIA INTERNATIONAL
Pynes Hill Court, Pynes Hill, Rydon Lane
Exeter, EX2 5AZ, United Kingdom
Tel: (+44) 1392 797680
E-mail: enquiries@fwmedia.com

SRN: S8737
ISBN-13: 978-1-44024-631-9

EDITOR: Maya Elson

TECHNICAL EDITOR: Debra Greenway

COVER DESIGNER: Elisabeth Lariviere

INTERIOR DESIGNER: Charlene Tiedemann

ILLUSTRATORS: Missy Shepler and Catherine Redford

PHOTOGRAPHERS: Christine Polomsky, Deana Travers, Dean Schoppner, and Hornick Rivlin Studio

Contents

HOW TO USE THIS BOOK.

This book is split into several sections to optimize learning how to quilt on your sewing machine.

First, it covers the basics of machine quilting and the materials, tools, and setup needed for success. Next comes the specifics of quilting with your walking foot—and not just in the ditch. Free-motion quilting follows with many designs drawn out so you can see clearly how I form the motifs. From there you can peruse a gallery of quilts I have made and quilted. It includes the design choices I made as I completed them to help inspire you to make your quilts uniquely yours. And finally, there are a few projects, suitable for you to practice your new skills, from small placemats to a large throw-size quilt.

This book was designed to be used as a journal on your quilting journey. Feel free to fill in your preferences on the tables throughout. Make notes in the margins. And when you try out something new, jot down your discoveries in the pages for future use. My hope is that this book will become a touchstone you can return to again and again as you become an even better quilter. **Welcome to** *Modern Machine Quilting!*

Introduction

I can't remember a time when I didn't make things.

I grew up in England, where knitting lessons started in second grade at school. But I learned from my grandma well before then. My mom taught home economics, and her best friend was a talented seamstress. Between the two of them, there was always a project in progress, and I wanted to join in. I was soon making clothes for my sister's Barbie dolls, moving on to my own clothes in junior high. I even made a flounced circular skirt when it became clear that stitching one myself was the only way I would ever own one!

I stitched wool needlepoint designs while studying for finals at college, sewed my own maternity clothes, and joined in with the cross-stitch craze in the early 1990s. Making was simply a constant in my life.

Life is either an adventure or nothing.
—HELEN KELLER

My family relocated to the United States in 1995. With four school-age children to look after and a whole new way of life to learn, I was glad to have any friends I could find, and the group just so happened to include a few quilters.

I got my introduction to quilting when my elder daughter joined the Girl Scouts. Her troop was making a quilt, so they went on a field trip to a local quilt shop, and I went along as a chaperone. That was a fateful day.

I booked a four-week beginner class at the store. We made a four-block sampler and handquilted it. I learned all about ¼" (6 mm) seams and nesting them together for accuracy. I signed up for my next class before I went home on the last day. I was hooked!

Quilt top followed quilt top. I soon realized that handquilting just wasn't going to work for finishing my quilts. I tied one quilt and that was quicker, but it's not suitable for every project. I needed to learn to machine quilt.

I took the shop's machine-quilting class. It was okay, but it wasn't really what I was looking for. I read some books and they helped a little. My new quilting friends were members of a quilt guild. I was a little intimidated, but I joined anyway. The guild had national speakers and teachers, and naturally, I signed up for as many classes as I could.

It was a class with master quilter Diane Gaudynski that finally made the difference. Her work was way out of my league, but she was patient and kind. By the end of the all-day class, I thought that with practice—make that years of practice—I might be able to at least become a competent machine quilter.

So, practice I did. I took more classes as opportunities arose. Each class taught me at least one new tip. In 2003, I was invited to start teaching myself, but I haven't stopped learning. Every new quilt I make is an opportunity to ask "what if?" and take a risk. I enjoy trying new designs and stitch combinations. The not-so-great quilts are an education, and the successful ones are another step forward in my quilting journey.

To keep a lamp burning we have to keep putting oil in it.
—MOTHER THERESA

Now I am a travelling quilt teacher. I'm living my dream. I love to teach and meet quilters on my expeditions. I'm writing this book to share my experiences, and I hope through it you learn something new that will stir your imagination and help you take one more happy step on your own creative journey.

Here's to finished quilts!
—CATHERINE

CHAPTER 1

Getting Started

Successful machine quilting starts
with the first thoughts you have about
your new project. The materials and
tools you choose play an important
role in turning those thoughts into a
beautiful finished quilt.

KEYS TO SUCCESS: MAKING GOOD CHOICES

I think a successful quilt starts at the planning stage. Some people begin with a few favorite fabrics and choose a pattern that shows them off to their best advantage. Others start with the pattern and then choose their fabrics. It doesn't really matter which way you do it, but do work with the best-quality fabrics you can afford and a pattern that fits the time frame you have in mind. Rushing against unreasonable time constraints can take all the joy out of piecing a quilt. It is so much kinder to yourself to have sensible expectations and enjoy the process.

Fabric

Most quilts are made from 100% cotton fabrics. I sometimes include fabrics containing some linen or other fibers. I like the added texture they can bring to a finished quilt top. Fabrics made from natural fibers are generally easier to sew and press.

Top-quality quilting cottons are printed on tightly woven, basic unfinished cloth, the *greige* goods. Good quilting cottons have a thread count of around 75, which makes them more stable and less prone to shrinkage than looser-weave cottons. Batiks have an even higher thread count that enables them to go through the whole batiking

A stack of beautiful solids and a few books, ready to inspire the next project.

process. The close weave helps prevent bearding (batting coming through your needle holes) when you are quilting.

The more expensive fabrics use more colorfast dyes and are finished with extra steps to set the dyes and make the fabric softer. This makes your piecing more accurate and your pressing easier.

When you are choosing fabrics for your next quilt, you might also look to see if the design was printed on grain. This is particularly important to make note of if the pattern has straight lines in it, or if you are cutting larger pieces, and you need the design to line up correctly along your seams.

Make sure to use at least the same quality of fabric for the back of your quilt as you use for the top. Bed sheets can seem like a good backing option because of their size, but they are often made of a very tightly woven cotton that can make it more difficult to get good machine-quilting results when you are sewing at high speed. I'll talk more about backing fabric choices later.

Considering all the time and effort you put into making a quilt, spending extra money for higher quality cloth is worthwhile. Purchasing first-class products on sale might be an option if you need to save a few pennies.

To Prewash or Not to Prewash?

I am quite open about my fabric washing habits! When I started quilting, I was taught to take all my fabric purchases home and wash them before I added them to my stash. I quickly realized that sometimes I was in too much of a hurry to use the fabric and didn't have time for this step. Then somebody told me that fabric-manufacturing standards had improved in recent years, and as long as I bought good-quality quilting fabrics, shrinkage and dye migration should be minimal. That was enough for me to stop prewashing my quilting fabrics!

Let me add the disclaimer that if I were planning an heirloom-quality quilt made out of red and white fabrics, I would wash all those fabrics before use.

Red is the dye color most likely to run, and I would feel that I should have known better if I made a two-colored Feathered Star quilt and the dyes ran in its first wash.

Also, some people are allergic to some of the fabric finishes, particularly those on batiks, so of course, they should wash all of their fabric purchases before use. You really just need to decide what works for you and go with that.

To Stash or Not to Stash?

When I first joined the quilting community, one of the wonderful things I discovered was the fabric stash. Shop hops were so much fun, and I loved the idea of having a carefully curated fabric palette ready for use. My stack of fat quarters grew rapidly as I bought more fabric than I could ever hope to use! Once I realized that sometimes a fat quarter just wasn't enough, I graduated to buying half yards of anything that took my fancy. Then there were the fabrics I might need for borders and backings. Some people said I should buy three yards, others said at least five.

Now that I've started working mostly in solids with fewer prints, I am reconsidering the whole stash idea. I really won't use all the fabric I have squirreled away. Some of my friends work hard to make scrappy quilts with all those amazing prints they have bought over the years, which is a great way to use up the fabric. But I have found a few good causes that will take quality fabric for various philanthropic ventures, and donating to them is helping me gradually reduce the amount of fabric I have stored.

So what do you do—stash, limited stash, or no stash? It's up to you! If you love the thrill of the chase and enjoy shopping the latest designer collections, it's certainly fun to build a stash that is always ready for when you find the perfect pattern. If you find your mind cluttered by an accumulation of stuff, it is fine to just buy what you need when you know you are going to use it. It is true that some colors go in and out of production, but if you are flexible, you can always find something super to use.

FORM & FUNCTION

All quilters enjoy the planning stage of making a quilt. Who doesn't love shopping for fabric? You flip through magazines, peruse books, maybe spend a few hours on Pinterest. . . . Finally you choose a design! And then you construct the quilt top. It might take a few hours or a few weeks, but after some careful cutting, stitching, and pressing, the top is complete.

What's next? It's not really a quilt until it's quilted.

Quilting adds form and function to your quilt. The function bit is easy. If it's a baby quilt, you know it's going to require frequent washing without falling to pieces. A wall quilt shouldn't sag when hung. Table runners or placemats need to lie flat so that bowls and plates won't tip over. A bed quilt needs to keep you warm.

Form might be slightly more difficult. It's the added design line you bring to your quilt by carefully choosing a quilting pattern. For example, if you are looking for a clean, modern look, then simple

straight lines might well fit the bill. Do you want your piecing to shine? An allover design that fades into the background and just adds texture could be what you need.

Once you start quilting your own quilts, you'll look for design inspiration everywhere. Quilt shows are a wonderful opportunity to note patterns that appeal to you. As you get more experience, you'll begin to come up with your own original ideas. Quilting your quilts might even become something you look forward to.

Good-quality batting makes all the difference when it comes to quilting your quilt. Make sure to read the instructions on the packet when you try a new batting.

Batting

When I started quilting, there weren't a lot of batting choices available, but that has changed. And now that there are many types of batting on the market, choosing the right batt for your project requires a little more research.

Loft, Drape, and Resilience

Words associated with batting include loft, drape, and resilience. Loft is essentially how fluffy the batting is, how high it is before it is quilted. Drape describes how stiff your quilted item will be. A table topper needs more drape than, say, a wall quilt, to hang nicely over a table. Resilience is how readily the batting goes back to its original shape. A quilt that is going to be folded for storage and then unfolded for

use needs to lose its creases quickly. This is particularly important for show quilts!

Color

Battings are available in different colors. If you are making a white quilt, then a white batt is a good idea, otherwise a natural, cream-colored batt is fine. A very dark quilt will benefit from a black batt, which will maintain the depth of color in your top.

Fiber Type

I prefer batting made from natural fibers. Unlike polyester batts, they breathe when used on a bed. Quilters Dream makes my favorite battings. They are beautifully even and soft and drape very nicely.

I usually use a 100% cotton batting. Battings come in different weights. I like Quilters Dream Cotton Request, which is a low-loft batting that is easy to maneuver through my domestic sewing machine. Quilters Dream Cotton Select is a slightly heavier batting that is good for a wall hanging, for example, to prevent sagging when it is displayed for extended periods of time.

Sometimes I use a wool batt. Wool is lofty but lightweight and washes very well. It has high resiliency and loses crease lines quickly. If I use flannel on the back of a baby quilt, for example, a wool batt counterbalances the added weight of the flannel fabric.

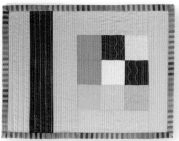

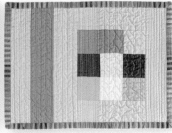

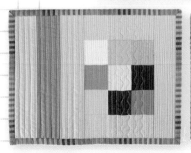

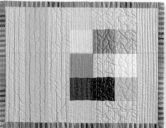

This set of placemats was constructed using cotton and wool battings for comparison before and after washing. The purple and dark green striped placemats use cotton batting, while the blue and light green striped placemats use wool batting. You can feel the difference if you handle them, but note how both shrank a similar amount. I do not prewash my fabrics. Perhaps the shrinkage has more to do with the fabric than the batting.

Batting	Composition	Line Spacing	Observations

Everyone has favorite battings. Note your personal observations in this table for future reference.

Polyester batts are an economical choice and can be a lighter weight than their cotton counterparts. Many quilters choose a cotton/polyester blend for their quilts to save money or to make a lighter-weight quilt.

Line Spacing

Most packages of batting come with directions about how far apart your quilting lines should be to avoid your batting disintegrating when it's washed. Battings are stabilized during manufacture by needle punching (felting), the addition of a scrim layer, or a combination of both. Quilting at the maximum distance will hold your quilt together, but won't be very decorative.

Right Side/Wrong Side

There is a right side to every batt. Whether how you orient your batt makes any difference to the look of your finished quilt is a matter of opinion. If you choose to use a fusible web to baste your top (some people do), you would need to put it with the right side to the back of your quilt top to avoid a lumpy finish. I just use safety pins so I don't really take much notice, but so you know, the right side is the side that the felting pins enter the batt during processing. This means that the right side is slightly smoother than the wrong side, which has little bumps of punched-through fibers.

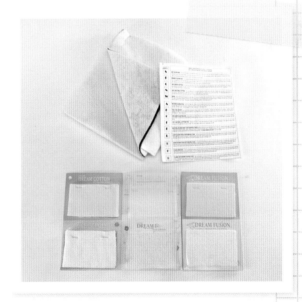

Batting samples are readily available from the major manufacturers. Look for them at national and regional quilt shows or contact the companies directly.

Sample Cards

Many manufacturers offer sample cards of their different battings. You can pick sample cards up at quilt shows and compare the different offerings. If you are curious about a particular batting, buy a small one and try it. It might be fun to join with your friends and make up a series of little quilts with different battings, wash them, and evaluate your results.

MAKING THE MOST OF YOUR BATTING

I like top-quality batting. Of course, it is a little bit more expensive than some of the economy brands. I save money by buying the largest packets available and cutting what I need as I go. This does mean that I have some odd pieces left over, but these can be great for smaller quilts, as in wall hangings or mini quilts.

There are several brands of fusible batting tapes on the market, which make joining those odd pieces together very easy (figure 1). Just butt the pieces next to each other, place the tape on top, adhesive-side down, and fuse with a quick pass of a warm iron, taking note of the individual manufacturer's instructions (figures 2 and 3). The tape is very soft and unobtrusive in your quilt sandwich (figure 4). I would use it in any

of my quilts other than a white quilt I might be expecting to enter in a show. (Those still get the first pieces cut from the package!)

Some batting is available on a roll, and this can be a cost-effective way to purchase large quantities. You do need to have a lot of room to store it, so this might not be an option for many quilters.

Figure 1   Batting tape makes joining odd pieces of batting easy and straightforward.

Figure 2   Line up the two pieces of batting to be joined on a pressing surface and lay the batting tape on top, fusible side down.

Figure 3   A quick press with a medium-hot iron is all you need to fuse the tape in place.

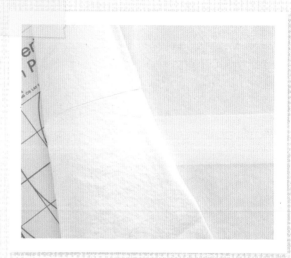

Figure 4   The joined batting is ready for use.

Thread

Your thread choices have a large impact on your quiltmaking experience. There are many great threads available, and using the right one for your purpose will affect everything from the accuracy of your piecing to the way your quilting line looks on your finished project.

Piecing Thread

Accurate piecing can be achieved more easily when you use a good-quality fine thread. A fine thread, e.g., #50 or #60 weight, allows you to sew a true ¼" (6 mm) seam allowance. I use the same thread in the top and the bottom when I piece, and this makes it easy to maintain good tension.

Quilting Thread

Your choice of quilting thread will make a significant difference to the look of your finished quilt. Many wonderful thread choices are available, and I use threads from many different manufacturers.

If you just want your quilting to add texture, choose a finer thread. I use a lot of Aurifil Cotton #50 weight thread and have also been using WonderFil's Deco Bob (#80 weight) and InvisiFil (#100 weight) threads. You can add a lot of quilting, backtracking if necessary over previous rows of stitching, without a build up of thread. Use a value (light, medium, or dark) similar to your quilt and you will see the texture without changing the color too much. The stitches will sink into your quilt top.

If you want the quilting to add color to your quilt, you will need to use a heavier-weight thread. Superior Threads' King Tut, Sulky's Cotton Blendables, Aurifil Cotton 28, and Wonderfil's Konfetti and Tutti threads all work well. These threads do not sink into your quilt but rather tend to lie on the surface. You will need to adjust the tension on your sewing machine for satisfactory results. Adding color will help blend fabrics together that you might have found too obtrusive in your top. You can also add a completely new design line for added interest.

I like to use a really heavy #12 weight thread to add a focal point or highlight. Aurifil Cotton #12 weight and WonderFil's Fruitti and Spagetti are my go-to threads for a very bold line.

TIP

Remember, the higher the number on your thread, the finer it is. The different thread manufacturers don't all use the same definition for the weight of their thread, but they will give you an indication of what to expect when you use them. You will often see two numbers on the spool, e.g., 50/2 or 50/3. The first number is the weight and the second is the ply. Three-ply is generally stronger than two-ply.

Fine thread makes for more accurate piecing.

NOTE

Some threads advertise themselves as long staple. This refers to the type of cotton used to make the thread. Some breeds of cotton plant produce bolls that have longer fibers or staples than others. A long staple is appreciated for the reduction in fuzzy ends on the spun thread and the corresponding reduction in lint when you sew with the thread. Extra-long staple is the highest quality thread available and produces very little lint, even when used at high speed in quilting.

Bobbin Thread

I usually use a fine thread on my bobbin and don't often change to something else. One bonus of doing this is that I don't have to wind as many bobbins as I would if I were to use the heavier thread! I usually use a #50 weight two-ply thread in my bobbin in a color that blends with my top thread.

NOTE

You might have some specialty threads in your thread stash. Almost anything can be used if you are careful. You just need to think about the eventual recipient of the quilt. If you are quilting a baby quilt, make sure whatever you use will stand up to repeated washings. If you are making an art quilt that will rarely or ever be laundered, washing is not an issue.

There are lots of thread choices for machine quilting. You will need to use a thread stand for the large cones of thread that are too big to go on top of your machine.

Thread	Preferred Needle	Observations

Here's a table to make a note of what works best for you. If you have found a favorite thread/needle combination, it's worth keeping a record for the next time.

Machine Needles

Different thread and fabric combinations need different needles. Choosing the right needle will make the whole stitching and quilting process much easier.

Changing Your Needle

I can't stress enough the importance of changing your sewing machine needle regularly. Some people say you should change your needle with every bobbin change, but I would go with changing your needle every six hours or so of sewing time. If you ever notice a clicking sound when stitching on your machine, chances are that you have a burr on your needle, and you need to change it right away. Occasionally, you will get a new needle that has a problem. Unfortunately, it will not improve with use. Buying a good-quality brand of needle will reduce the chances of a faulty needle.

Sharpness

I always use sharp needles for piecing my quilts. There was a time when all fabrics were woven and all sewing machine needles were "sharp." With the advent of knitted fabrics, there was a new need for ballpoint needles with a blunted round tip to avoid shredding the fibers of these new fabrics. Manufacturers came up with a Universal needle that could be used for both woven and knitted fabrics. These needles are okay but not the best for either purpose. It is much better to use a ballpoint needle for knitted fabric and a sharp needle for woven fabric.

When it comes to piecing your quilts, using a sharp needle will give you straighter lines and therefore more accurate blocks. When quilting, there will be fewer problems with skipped stitches as the needle will pierce your quilt cleanly.

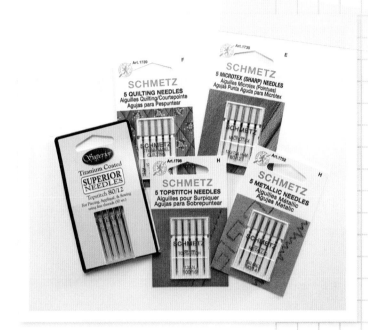

Choose a sharp-tipped needle in the right size for your thread and fabrics.

TIP

I find a sharp needle in the correct size to be good enough for most situations. I do sometimes use the titanium-coated topstitching needles produced by Superior Threads. If you are having problems, try a different needle and see if it helps. Different machines work better with different needles. It's worth trying a few needles to see what you prefer—and remember to change your needle regularly!

Sizes

Needles come in different sizes; the larger the number, the bigger the diameter of the sewing machine needle. I like to choose a needle with a big-enough eye for the thread to go through easily but not so fat that it makes holes in your fabric that the thread doesn't fill. If the needle is too big, you will be able to see through your quilt if you hold it up to the light.

However, if you use too small a needle, then you will have problems with thread breakage as the thread rubs against the eye during sewing. The thread goes backward and forward through the eye of the needle over thirty times before it becomes a stitch. The resulting friction from a small eye easily breaks a fine thread. This problem is worse when you run your machine fast. Choosing your needle size is a balance between making a small-enough hole to be filled by the thread going through it and the eye being big enough not to fray the thread. An embroidery needle or topstitch needle with an elongated eye will also help. Metallic needles have a special friction-reducing coating to further diminish the effect. Quilting needles are strengthened to be extra sharp and strong to handle the layers of fabric at seam intersections without bending.

TIP

Remember, whatever make or model of machine you have, they all benefit from being kept clean and oiled. Check with your dealer to make sure you understand what is appropriate for your machine. Regular tune-ups from a reputable mechanic will keep your machine purring and extend its life. Treat your machine with care, and it will repay you with reliable service.

Sewing Machine

I quilt all my quilts on a domestic sewing machine. Long- and mid-arm quilting machines are becoming increasingly popular with the home quilter, but they are an expensive addition to the family budget and take up a lot of space!

Domestic machines come in many shapes and sizes and at many different price points. If you are thinking of investing in a new piece of equipment, your budget might be your first consideration. I don't think anyone should go into debt for a sewing machine! That being said, machine quality does vary considerably between models and brands, and you do get what you pay for. Make sure you take a test drive before making any purchase and sign up for all the lessons your local dealer offers.

Take samples of the projects you are likely to want to stitch and try the machine at the speed you are hoping to run it. If you intend to use your new machine for free-motion quilting, make sure you can make smooth, tight curves and circles without the tension slipping. For successful free-motion quilting, the machine needs to be capable of fully completing each stitch in whatever direction you are moving the quilt sandwich. Unfortunately, not every machine on the market is able to do this, and it can be disappointing to find that out in the middle of your carefully planned project.

If your budget affords it, I would look for extras such as a needle-down option and a hands-free system (knee lift or hover). Both of these are like having a second set of hands and make a positive difference to my sewing experience. Being able to lower your presser-foot pressure and having as big a throat space as you can get are also a great help to achieve successful stitching. Good built-in lighting on the machine is great but can be easily enhanced. I don't use the thread cutter or the needle threader! Hundreds of stitch variations and embroidery capabilities are not of great interest to me, but some people like them and are willing to pay for them.

I own a machine with an integrated dual-feed system. It is an even-feed system that works as a built-in walking foot. My machine has a variety of feet that can be used with the system engaged, adding greatly to visibility and versatility when stitching. It's a pricey extra but is well worth it to me.

I don't use a stitch regulator. I know lots of people who do and love using them. A stitch regulator reads the number of threads passing under it to automatically regulate the length of your stitches when free-motion quilting. Not using this device is a little like driving a stick shift in that without it one is able to have finer control over the stitches. And using a stitch regulator is a little like driving an automatic transmission; it certainly shortens the learning curve of free-motion quilting, but it will never give you the same control of your machine as sewing without one.

If you are planning to travel with your machine, either to classes or retreats, then you will want to consider its weight. I have a smaller machine that I take outside the house but that still gives me the capacity for accurate piecing and painless quilting. A used machine from a reputable dealer might be a good solution if you are looking for a second machine.

Buying a new sewing machine can be a lot of fun and is certainly not something we do every day, so take your time and enjoy the process. Coming home with the right sewing machine for you is a satisfying experience with lots of potential for some wonder-filled days ahead!

Pressing sprays, finger guards, and a pressing stick make pressing your seams easier and safer.

TOP SIX STEPS TO SANDWICH SUCCESS

1. Measure and pin when sewing long strips together.

2. Press carefully, whether you choose to press your seams to one side or open.

3. Make sure the backing is flat.

4. Tape the backing to secure the surface before placing the batting and the quilt top.

5. Check that your seams are straight before starting to pin.

6. Pin baste with plenty of pins.

PREPARING THE QUILT SANDWICH

The quilt sandwich has three layers: the top, the batting, and the backing. Each layer is important for quilting success. We have already considered the batting, but let's take a look at the top and the backing and the tools and techniques you'll use on your way to putting it all together.

The Quilt Top

Careful construction of your quilt top really will make a difference when you come to quilting it. Make sure that all your seams are even and secure, and your pressing is flat. "Quilting it out" just does not work! I really do not like to pin when I am piecing, but whenever I am stitching strips longer than 12" (30.5 cm), I pin carefully to make sure the seam will lie smoothly. Borders must always be measured and pinned before sewing.

Remember to trim your long threads as you go. If you leave them hanging, they will peep through your quilt when it's basting time, and you won't know if they were important until you try pulling on one and have your stitching line come undone!

Pressing

Pressing is different from ironing. When I press my quilt blocks, I use more of a simple downward pressure on the fabrics than the backward and forward motion that I might use while ironing a shirt.

Whether you choose to press your seams open or closed, you need to make sure that the front is completely flat and there are no tucks. I start by pressing my seams from the back while they are still closed to set the seams and to release any tension the stitching introduced.

If I am pressing my seams to one side, I then turn the block over and work exclusively from the top, lifting the upper piece of fabric away from me and carefully pressing the seam line. That way the ditches are opened up, and my work will be smooth.

Open seams need to be approached from the back, carefully opening the seam ahead of the tip of the iron. A pressing stick, similar to a half round from your local DIY store but with a nice smooth finish, really helps. It lifts the seam you are pressing away from the rest of your seams and aids in avoiding catching your other seams as you go.

A final front pressing is essential for accurate work.

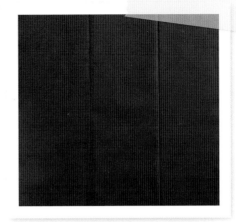

Pressing your seams open (left seam) will make for a flatter quilt top than one where the seams are pressed to one side (right seam).

Press each seam after stitching while it is still closed.

Press to one side: Working from the top, flip the fabric to one side and press along the seam line

Press open: Carefully run your finger along the seam ahead of the iron. Use a pressing stick to help open the seam and raise it above any others surrounding it.

TIP

Remember to be careful not to catch your fingertips with the hot iron. If you want extra protection against burns, you can get silicone finger guards that will help.

A pieced backing

The Quilt Backing

Your quilt back, the third layer in your sandwich, should be made of fabric that is at least as good a quality as the quilt top itself. The back needs to be a minimum of 2" (5 cm) bigger than your quilt top all the way around to make it easier to baste and to give you something to hold onto when you are quilting the edges of your quilt. This is a smaller allowance than a longarm quilter will ask for. They need the extra allowance for their clamps and pins.

Some people like to piece their backings from left-over blocks or fabric from the quilt top. If your top measures more than 42" (106.5 cm) on its smallest side, you will need to piece your backing unless you buy a nonstandard quilting fabric. Quilt backing fabric that is up to 120" (305 cm) wide is available in many quilt stores. However you choose to construct your backing, make sure it is squared off at the ends just as neatly as your quilt top. This will be important when it comes to basting your quilt.

If you are concerned about your stitch quality, remember that a small scale, busy print on the back of your quilt will hide a multitude of sins! By all means, choose a plain fabric if you plan to change your bobbin thread with all your top thread changes, and you want people to be able to appreciate your effort.

You might also like to try one of the various Minky or Cuddle stretchy microfiber fleece fabrics. Used with care, they are very soft and warm for a special cuddly quilt. Flannel fabrics are less stretchy and can also be used for a nice soft backing.

If your quilt top is very light in color, take care when choosing your backing. A dark fabric or one with a high-contrast design might show through your batting. Remember to check for this before you go to all the effort of basting your quilt!

Marking

Whatever type of quilt I am going to stitch, my favorite kind of marking is no marking! However, there are times when some marking is necessary to achieve the desired result. Some varieties of marking are added before you baste your quilt sandwich. Other types can be done on an as-needed basis as your quilting progresses.

Painter's Tape

I often use painter's tape to mark a straight line across a quilt top. I prefer the low-tack blue tape, but regular masking tape works well too, as long as it is removed immediately after use. I always place the tape an even distance away from my intended stitching line (e.g., a presser-foot width away) so I can just run the edge of my sewing machine foot along it and avoid stitching through the tape, which will gum up your machine needle and make it unusable. Painter's tape comes in different widths, so you can find the width that works best for you. It can be removed and reused several times before you need a new piece.

Hera Marker or Stiletto

The sharp point of a hera marker or stiletto can be used to make a crease in your quilt top for a clear line you can see in good light.

Chalk Pencil

There are many brands of chalk pencil available to quilters. Look for one that is grease-free so that there is no line left when the chalk is brushed off. Chalk refills can be purchased in several different colors to be visible on different-colored fabrics. Make sure to check that they don't leave a stain on the fabrics you are using before you use them on your quilt top. I prefer the chalks that come in a mechanical pencil format and make very fine lines. The white chalk lasts just long enough to complete your stitching before it brushes off.

Air-Erasable/Water-Erasable Pens

Quilters have lots of options for erasable pens. Some are described as air-erasable. These marks dissipate over time into the air. They disappear very quickly in humid conditions. Marks from water-erasable pens disappear when moistened with water. I have spoken to several manufacturers of these pens, and they confirmed my suspicions that that there is always some residue left behind in your quilt unless you rinse it away by completely submersing your finished quilt in water. If you intend to wash your quilt, this is not a problem, but if you are making an art quilt from delicate fibers, it is something to bear in mind.

Heat-Erasable Pens

Heat-erasable pens should also be used with caution. Make sure to try them out on a fabric sample before use to check for a reaction between their ink and the dyes in your quilt. These pens were designed for use with paper and their ink can bleach some fabrics. You should also rinse the residues away as some of the ink has been shown to come back if the quilt gets very cold. This might be an issue for a quilt that isn't going to be washed before shipping.

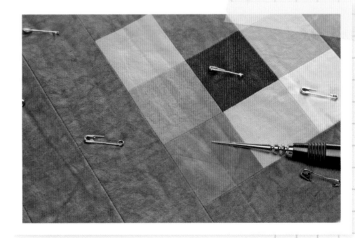

Making a crease with a stiletto or hera marker against a straight edge can be an easy and effective way of making a temporary mark on your quilt.

Basting

Basting is probably my least favorite part of making a quilt. That being said, it is very important not to rush it. I pin baste my quilts. I know some people use basting sprays with a good degree of success. My attempts at spray basting have resulted in messy overspray, and I don't like the smell. If you do spray baste, take care to work in a well-ventilated area and follow the manufacturer's directions carefully. Stitch basting is not a good idea for machine quilting because the basting thread tends to get stuck in the machine stitching and is difficult to remove.

Some manufacturers have introduced fusible battings. The ones I have tried have worked well for small quilts, but I found them difficult to handle for larger quilts. In particular, I struggled to keep everything straight during the ironing steps required for fusing the layers together.

Pin Basting

1. Make sure to press your backing well before you lay it right side down on your table (Figure 1).

2. Next, you'll need to secure the backing. I use a mix of binder clips and painter's tape to make it tight but not too taut on the table. If it springs back when you remove the tape, it's too tight. I

> **TIP**
>
> The surface you choose for basting your quilt really can make a difference! I am able to baste large quilts on a standard-size table. I used to baste my quilts on the floor, but since I started using a table, I am much more accurate and have been able to use striped and directional fabrics for my backings quite successfully.

Binder clips, 1" (2.5 cm) curved safety pins, and a Kwik Klip™ are my favorite tools for successful basting.

use the edges of my table to line up the backing and keep it straight (Figure 2). (If your quilt is bigger than the top of your table, line up the top and one side to the edges of the table and allow the extra fabric to fall over the other sides before using binder clips on those edges.)

3. Spread your batting out on top of the backing (Figure 3). Take care not to stretch the batting. If your batting has been folded in a plastic bag, it will have creases in it. Pat the creases out rather than pulling on them. A few minutes on the air-fluff cycle in your clothes dryer can help with particularly stubborn creases, or you could try some careful pressing with a little steam.

4. Give your top one final press and then lay it on top of the batting. Position the top about 2" (5 cm) in from the edge of the table, starting in the left-hand corner you lined up previously. There should be at least 1" (2.5 cm) of batting showing around the quilt top. Use long rulers to make sure the seams are straight and adjust accordingly (Figure 4).

Figure 1

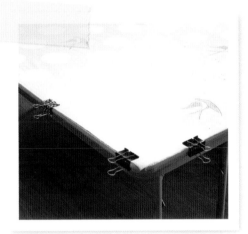

Figure 2

Figure 3

Figure 4

5. Keeping the top flat with your fingers as you go, start pinning the layers together using good quality 1" (2.5 cm) safety pins. (Figure 5) Begin in the center of the area you are basting and leaving no more than 3" (7.5 cm) between pins. (Figure 6) Offset each row, and leave the pins open until a large area is completed (i.e., the whole of the top that is on the table until you are about 9" (23 cm) from the overhang. [Figure 7]). I don't worry about avoiding seam lines; keeping a good distance between the pins is more important.

6. Close the pins, taking care not to shift the layers. Use a Kwik Klip™ tool to help with the closing (Figure 8). A large quilt requires several hundred pins for basting, and closing them all can make your fingers sore.

7. If your quilt is large, finish pinning the area on top of your table and then remove your binder clips and tape before repositioning your layers and continuing pinning in the next area. (Figure 9)

8. Once your pinning is finished, trim the batting and backing as necessary. (Figure 10)

Figure 5

Figure 6

Figure 7

Figure 8

Figure 9

TIP

Curved safety pins are a small luxury that makes inserting the pins a little easier, but they aren't strictly necessary!

Figure 10

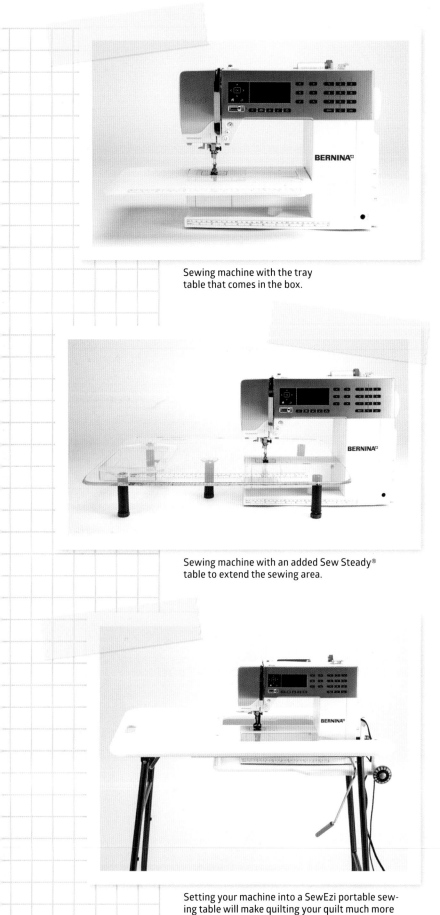

Sewing machine with the tray table that comes in the box.

Sewing machine with an added Sew Steady® table to extend the sewing area.

Setting your machine into a SewEzi portable sewing table will make quilting your quilt much more comfortable when space is at a premium.

QUILT ROOM SETUP

Not many of us have the luxury of a dedicated sewing room with specially designed furniture for our machine. If you have a custom cabinet, you know how wonderful it is to have your machine set down at table level with lots of space around it to support your work.

But if you don't have a dream setup, there is plenty you can do to create a comfortable quilting environment. It is certainly worth taking the extra time and effort to arrange your sewing space before you start stitching.

Table Options

Whatever table setup you choose, your goal should be to support the weight of your quilt to stop it pulling down and help it feed smoothly through your machine.

Start with any slide-on table that comes with your machine to extend the space around your needle. This will help you with your piecing, but unless your machine came with a special quilting package, it is unlikely that it will come with a table that gives you sufficient space for quilting.

An acrylic add-on extension table, such as those made by Sew Steady®, works very well for many people. You need to buy one with a cutout specific to your machine and use your machine on top of a regular table. Sew Steady® tables are very easy to store if you have space constraints. The only problem is that your machine will be set quite high, so if you are not very tall, you will find that you need a height-adjustable chair to have a clear view of your work. Then it can be difficult to reach your foot pedal! Try an old-style telephone directory or maybe a toddler step to raise the pedal if you have this problem.

A portable sewing machine table like the one from SewEzi is another way to extend the space around your needle for quilting. This table comes with a machine-specific insert and folds up for storage. Your machine bed will be at normal table height, which means that you can use a regular chair. You can place the table next to a second table to further extend the space around your machine and support your work while you are sewing.

Of course, a good cabinet with space at both sides and behind your machine is the number one solution. And it works best when you keep all that extra space clear! I try to keep all the extensions on mine folded down when I don't need them for sewing to avoid the temptation to use them as a dumping ground for all the stuff I continually accumulate in my sewing room. If you have a cabinet and it doesn't have extensions, try putting an ironing board set to the right height next to you on the left-hand side to provide extra support, or work next to a wall so that the quilt doesn't slip off.

Chair

Be kind to yourself and get a good ergonomically designed chair. You need to be comfortable and relaxed when you are sitting at your sewing machine. The wrong chair leads to bad posture, causing back and shoulder pain. Your chair should allow your feet to reach the ground and use the foot pedal easily without overstretching. The backrest should support the natural curve of your spine to avoid slouching! There are many good chairs available on the market. Be sure to find one that suits you. If you are on a carpeted surface, it is nice to put your wheeled chair on a plastic mat for effortless movement. The mat will also make it much easier to keep the area around your sewing space clean.

Lighting

Good lighting makes all the difference to your work. There are all sorts of supplementary lights available for machine sewing that attach to your machine. I like to have a daylight lamp with an adjustable neck that I can shine at just the right angle to see what I'm doing. A good pair of glasses prescribed just for stitching helps, too!

Storage

Adequate storage might not seem to be part of a good setup for successful machine quilting, but there's something about a clean and tidy studio that really makes a difference. I started out with stackable plastic tubs, but somehow the fabric I wanted always seem to be in the bottom container. I use a system of mesh drawers now and that helps a lot. I still have to be disciplined about tidying as I go. . . . I can always dream!

Setting your machine in a large table will make quilting a large quilt much less stressful. Having a good chair at the right height makes a lot of difference. Notice how the quilt is supported all the way around so that it does not pull against the machine while you are stitching.

A shot of Catherine's Studio.

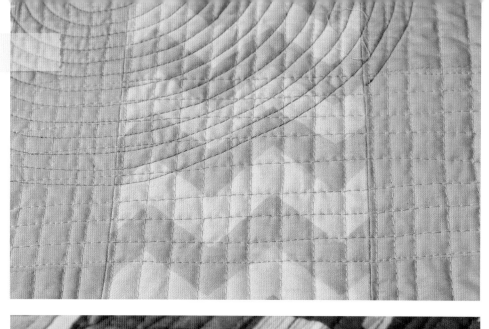

CHAPTER 2

Walking-Foot Quilting

With the rise of the modern-quilting aesthetic, interest in walking-foot quilting has increased. A walking foot can easily create the linear quilting designs that enhance the clean look of a modern quilt. In this chapter, along with the basics of walking-foot quilting, I present some new ideas and fine-tuned basic skills for getting consistent results. They are easy to learn and to adapt to your own particular style.

MACHINE SETUP BASICS

Before you can begin quilting, you need to make sure your machine is set up with the right attachments for the task ahead.

The Walking Foot

Unless your machine comes with a built-in even-feed system, you will need a walking foot for walking-foot quilting. During normal sewing, the feed dogs in your machine grip the bottom layer of your sewing and take it under the needle. You might pin your layers together or just hold them to make sure the top layer of fabric goes through, too. Even so, you may have noticed when you piece long strips together that the bottom fabric goes through faster, and what started as two strips the same size ends up with a little bit left over on top. You can use this to your advantage if you want to ease a little bit of extra fabric into a seam. Just put the longer piece on the bottom and let your machine do the work.

When you add a walking foot to your machine, or engage a dual- or even-feed system, then you are adding the equivalent of a top set of feed dogs. Both feed systems work together to take the layers through evenly. Good basting techniques will ensure that the batting is taken through, too, and you will get a quilt without puckers and tucks.

Walking feet are usually machine-specific, so make sure you get the right one for your machine. Read the instructions for how to put the walking foot on properly. It can be a little awkward to put the foot on your machine and make sure the arm is in the right place, but it gets easier with practice. Making sure the foot is raised to its highest level will give you the maximum amount of space for maneuvering.

I like to use a foot with an open-toe sole plate, so I can see in front of the needle. If there is a bar in front, it can be difficult to see where you are going. Some feet come with replaceable soles, so you have a choice, depending on the type of sewing you want to do. Many feet come with seam guides that you can attach to help with your accuracy.

All walking feet are big and clunky, so when I use my machine that has an integrated dual feed, I just use that instead. I find it works as well as the walking foot, and it is much easier to see where I'm going.

Single-Hole Stitch Plate

I have a single-hole stitch plate for my machine, and I put that on when I know I am going to be sewing straight lines without moving my needle position. The small hole supports your fabric as it passes under the moving needle, making a cleaner stitch and a straighter line.

However, if I know I am going to be moving my needle from the center or using other stitches, I don't change the plate, as the benefits I get are outweighed by breaking needles when I forget it's there! I could use my machine's security devices to remind me, but not everyone has those available.

GETTING STARTED

Once my quilt sandwich is ready for stitching, I make sure my machine is clean and oiled, a suitable sharp needle is in place, and my work surface is clear. I check my stitch length and adjust my tension on a small quilt sandwich made from the same fabric and batting as my actual quilt.

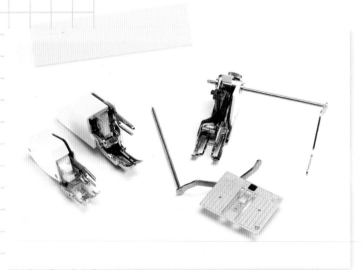

Contact your dealer to purchase the correct walking foot for your machine. A single-hole stitch plate will improve the quality of your straight stitches.

Checking Your Tension

You might be feeling tense as you approach your sewing machine, so take a few deep breaths and know that everything is well with the world and nobody is forcing you to stitch. . . . You have chosen to do this!

Of course, what I'm really referring to here is the all-important machine tension. If you have the same type of thread in the top and bottom of your machine, chances are that you won't need to make adjustments to your machine's tension in order to get a nice even stitch. Basically you are looking for your stitch to look the same on both sides of the quilt sandwich. Your threads should meet somewhere in the middle with no little loops showing on either side.

If you have a loop of the bottom thread showing on the top over a tight-looking top thread, then your top tension is too tight. Loosen it by turning the appropriate dial to a lower number.

If the reverse is happening and there are loops of the top thread showing on the back, then you'll need to tighten your top tension by choosing a higher number to pull a little harder on that top thread.

You can think of it as a tug-of-war where there are cheerleaders on one side and a football team on the other. Under most circumstances the football players are going to pull the cheerleaders across the

Front side of stitched-out sample with tension set at 9 (left-hand side) to 1 (right-hand side). White thread is on top, purple on the back.

Back side of stitched-out sample. Look for good tension, where very little top thread is seen on the back and very little bottom thread is seen on the front.

Top Thread	Bobbin Thread	Tension Setting	Observations

Make note of your tension settings for future use.

center marker, but if you add some reinforcement to the weaker side, then you can even up the odds!

You don't want to discover a tension problem while you are stitching on your carefully pieced quilt, so keep some sample quilt sandwiches next to your machine, ready to use to check your tension every time you change your thread or put in a new bobbin. The sample sandwich should use the same fabrics and batting as the quilt you are working on.

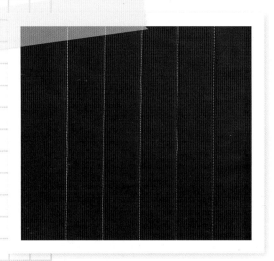

Make a sample piece using your favorite threads.

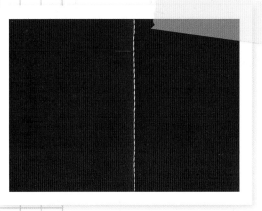

Five small stitches make a secure start or stop to your quilting line

It takes a long time to remove bad or faulty quilting, so this extra step is really worthwhile.

With wildly different threads on each side, more modification might be necessary, even to the point of changing the tension on your bobbin case. I'd recommend looking at your machine's user guide before you try this. You might also want to take a trip to your dealer for advice.

If after adjustment your machine still struggles, use the same color thread on the top and in the bobbin, so any loops won't draw attention to themselves.

Keep notes of the needle you used, your stitch length, and any tension adjustments you needed to make.

Where to Start Stitching?

I guess that is the million-dollar question. All the while I am making a quilt top, from initially drawing it out on graph paper to the final seam, I am thinking about how I am going to quilt it. This usually means I have a plan by sewing time.

If I am going for an allover straight line or grid design, I will start near the middle of my quilt and work out toward one edge before turning my quilt around and heading out to the other side. If you have problems with your quilt top dragging as you sew, try adjusting your presser-foot pressure. If your machine does not have this capability, you might need to alternate the direction of each sewing line.

More complicated designs might involve some stabilization before you add different designs to separate sections of your quilt. I might do some stitching in the ditch right at the beginning of the quilting process, before proceeding.

Smooth Stops and Starts

I think of stops and starts while making a quilt like hill starts in stick-shift driving.

I try to keep thread stops and starts to a minimum. If I can, I use the edges of the quilt for most of them so they will be under the binding. I prefer an edge-to-edge design wherever possible.

If I do need to start in the middle of my piece, then I will pull up my bottom thread and make five small stitches before continuing with my normal stitch length. You can either set your stitch length to a very short stitch to do this or hold your quilt firmly with your hands, allowing it to move very slightly to make five stitches in the normal length of one. Some people set this in their machine's memory, so they toggle over to it quite easily. I finish in a similar fashion with five small stitches before trimming my threads. I find this is quite sufficient to secure my quilting. If I am using a heavier-weight thread, this method doesn't work, and I bury my threads using a self-threading hand-sewing needle.

Start stitching with five small stitches to secure your line when you start away from the edge of your quilt. If you have places where you need to leave a gap in the stitching, finish with five small stitches, lift your presser foot to make the jump, and start again with another set of small stitches.

Choosing Your Stitch Length

Your sewing machine sets the stitch length as the length of thread between each intersection of the top and bottom thread. This means that the same setting used for regular stitching will result in a longer stitch than when you are quilting through batting. The stitch will appear shorter in a thicker batting. If I am using a combination of free-motion stitching and walking-foot quilting in the same quilt, I adjust my stitch length for the walking-foot portion to match my usual free-motion stitch length. This varies between quilters, so you will need to make some trial pieces to find what works for you.

TIP

If you stabilized your quilt sandwich properly with safety pins, you should be able to steer it through your machine with a minimum of pushing and pulling. Set your machine to stop in its needle-down position if you can. Resist the temptation to move your hands while your foot is on the pedal! Whenever you get to a pin, stop and take it out. This is where it's good if you have some of your pins in the way. Take the opportunity to reposition your hands and set off again, keeping your hands on either side of your stitching and at the front of the machine.

Make a sample with your chosen thread to choose a stitch length you find pleasing. You might like to increase your stitch length with heavier threads and choose a shorter stitch length when you are using a very fine thread.

Pulling Up the Bottom Thread

I was taught to have both threads in my left hand whenever I start stitching. This avoids unsightly birds' nests on the back of my work. But if you are starting off a distance away from the edge of your quilt, you can't do this unless you pull the bottom thread up to the top.

To pull the bottom thread up, make sure you have your top thread secure in your hand and take just one stitch with the needle going down into the sandwich and back out again, right to its highest position. Release the tension by raising the presser foot and gently tug on the top thread. You should see a loop coming through to the front of your top. This is the bottom thread. Carefully pull it through to the front. Now you can start sewing with both threads securely held in your hand and no bird's nest! This is where a hands-free system or knee lift really comes in handy. It's also the reason I don't use the automatic thread cutter on my machine, as the cutter trims the back thread too close to pull through easily.

1 Hold the top thread.

2 Take one stitch in.

3 Take one stitch out of the fabric sandwich.

4 Lift the presser foot and pull forward on the top thread to bring the back loop up.

5 Hold both threads as you lower the presser foot and begin stitching for a neat start to your work.

Jumping Across Small Gaps

This is a good practice because quilters need all the exercise they can get!

But seriously, when I come to the end of a stitching line in the middle of my quilt and I need to start again just a short distance away, I finish the first line with small stitches, bring the needle to the top, release the tension, and slide my quilt to the new starting place where I begin again with more small stitches. I go back and trim the jumping thread later.

If the gap is bigger (more than 2" [5 cm]), I finish the first line, bring the thread up to the top, and cut the thread before restarting in the usual way.

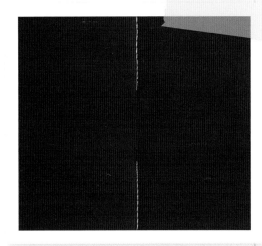

Trim your jumping thread later to make a neat line.

TIP

Remember most sewing machines are designed to stitch well through two layers of fabric. You might need to adjust your tension to make a good clean stitch when stitching through your quilt sandwich.

STITCHING OVER NESTED SEAMS

If you are stitching in the ditch over pieced seams, you will come to horizontal breaks where you need to switch sides to stay on the lower side of the seam. Assuming your seams are nested nicely, you will find it very easy to do. If you have a slight gap where your seams didn't quite match, stop at the horizontal seam and raise your needle. Slide your work across to the new vertical seam and start again. Your thread will disappear in the crosswise seam, looking as if you took a perpendicular stitch. If the gap is longer than one stitch length, you might want to consider a different finishing option.

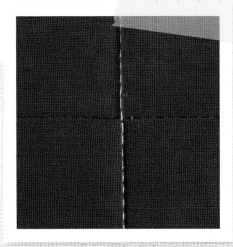

When you are stitching in the ditch and you come to a nested seam, your stitching almost automatically switches sides to stay on the low side of the seam.

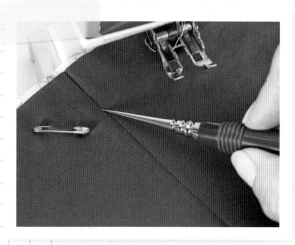

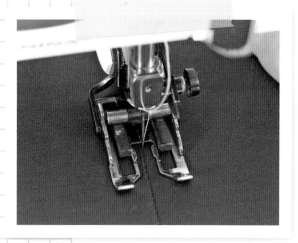

1 Run down your seam line with a stiletto or ballpoint awl just before stitching to completely open the ditch.

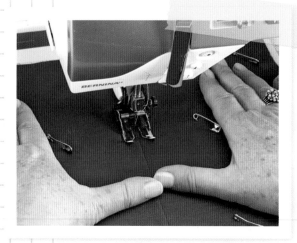

2 Sew on the low side of the seam. That is the side you pressed away from when you were constructing your quilt top.

3 Hold your hands on either side of the seam line, flat against the quilt, in a "hoop" whenever possible.

STRAIGHT LINES

We've covered lots of details, now it really is time to start stitching in earnest. Straight lines will unify your patchwork design.

Stitching in the Ditch

Traditionally, many quilters seem to equate walking-foot quilting with stitching in the ditch, a technique that involves stitching as close to the seam line (the ditch) as possible. Machine quilters may have adopted this technique to imitate hand quilting, which historically was often placed right next to the seams. While the ditch might be a great place for a hand stitcher to sew, it can be very difficult for machine quilters to keep close to the seam. A few stitches taken off either way and the stitching shows.

While stitching in the ditch certainly adds function to a quilt by helping to stabilize it, but doesn't necessarily add much in the way of form or design. The quilt will be useable but isn't any prettier! Although my advice would be to "get out of the ditch!" whenever possible, I do have some tips to help make stitching in the ditch easier.

Assuming you have carefully pressed your seams to one side from the front, you will have a nice ditch to sew in. Be sure to sew on the low side of the seam; that's the side you pressed away from. Start at the top of your seam and stitch slowly and carefully. Stop every time you need to move your hands to avoid jogs. Remember to remove your pins as you go.

My best tip for success is to run down the seam line with a stiletto just before you sew. This will open up the ditch so you can get in really close. With practice and a closely matched thread, your stitching will virtually disappear. I don't like to use so-called invisible thread because I find any stray stitches catch the light and show up more than a matching colored thread.

With practice, stitching in the ditch is barely visible, even when sewn with white thread on a purple background.

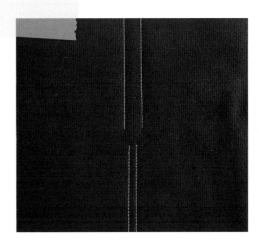

You can choose your own preferred distance for shadow quilting either side of the seam line.

Shadow Quilting

If you like to press your seams open, then you have no ditches to stitch inside. If you want to follow your seam lines, you need to shadow or echo quilt. This just means you will be stitching to one side of your seams probably at least ⅛" (3 mm) away. If I am shadow quilting, I like to stitch down both sides of the seam line. This adds a lot of strength to the seam. Even if the quilt is washed frequently, there will be no pull on the construction stitching. So shadow quilting adds a lot of function to your quilt, and I think the double line adds more to the design than a single line manages on its own.

Even when my seams are pressed to one side, I usually choose to shadow quilt, rather than stitch in the ditch. The only time I stay in the ditch these days is when I want to stabilize seam lines before I add more stitching. I might stabilize the quilt top, removing all the safety pins, if I have a complex quilting design in mind. The initial ditch stitching will fade into the background under the busy stitching patterns

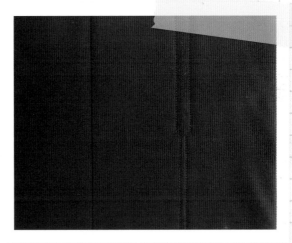

Stitching with a matching thread shows how the ditch stitching disappears and the shadow quilting lines just add texture to your quilt.

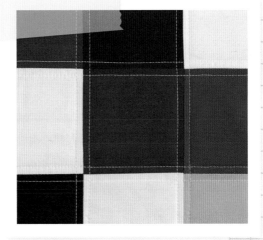

Shadow or echo quilting each seam adds function and a second design line.

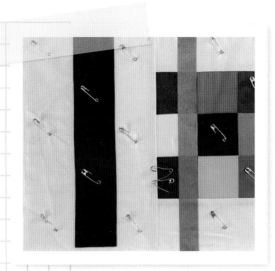

Painter's tape is useful to mark your starting line, particularly if your seams do not reach the edges of your quilt.

Star block with simple shadow quilting to add function and a little form.

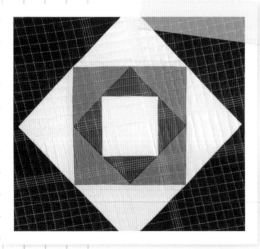

Square in a square block with offset irregular grid to add function and a completely separate secondary design.

Parallell Lines

You can add a lot of texture to your quilt using just straight lines. Many modern quilts look great with allover parallel straight lines. They unify the design and maintain a clean aesthetic.

If possible, I start my lines by shadow stitching one complete seam on my quilt. If there are no suitable seam lines to follow, I usually use a piece of painter's tape as a guide. Make sure you place the tape so that you can use the edge of your walking foot alongside the edge of the tape.

Do not plan on stitching right next to the tape. It is too easy to stray, and if you allow your needle to make one stitch through the tape, it will be gummed up and need replacing.

Once I have made that first line, I use the edge of my foot for the second line and just work out to the side of my quilt. Sometimes I will place another piece of tape to help me keep my lines straight.

TIP

Handling a big quilt can be done quite successfully if you are patient. I generally start near the center and work out to one side before turning the quilt around and stitching the other side. I roll up the bulk of the quilt on the right-hand side to go through the machine and gradually unroll it as I get nearer the edge. The part of the quilt to the left of the needle needs to be supported as much as possible. This is where you will be glad to have a big cabinet, or an extra table, or even an ironing board next to you while you work.

As I approach the tape, I will gradually make the necessary adjustments. I tend not to worry about making my lines perfectly even or perfectly parallel. After all, it's me, not a computer-guided machine, doing the quilting.

If my seams have been pressed open, I will avoid stitching in the seam line. This might mean that I have two lines a little closer together or a little farther apart, but I don't see that as a problem.

If the quilt is small, you can turn it around at the end of each line and stitch in both directions. For larger quilts, you will need to go back to the top to start stitching each time. If you are having problems with drag across the horizontal lines of your piecing, try reducing your presser-foot pressure. That usually helps!

POSITIONING YOUR HANDS

I generally advise people to keep their hands in a hoop-like position when they are machine quilting, and this works well most of the time. However, there are situations when you need to get a firmer grip on your work: if the quilt just isn't moving well, you are near the edge of your work, or it just feels better. Do whatever works for you!

Some people find holding their hands in a hoop position works well.

Sometimes having one hand flat and the other hand holding a portion of the quilt works. Find what works for you!

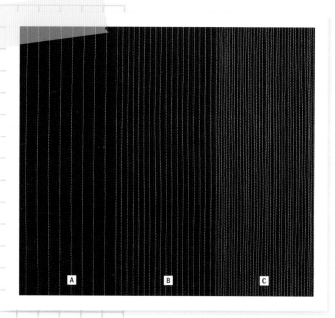

Building up the lines for matchstick quilting: Start by stitching across your top using the edge of your foot for spacing [A]. Next, stitch down the center of each space [B]. Finish by stitching between each of those lines for closely stitched lines around ⅛" (3 mm) apart [C].

Matchstick Quilting

I really like the look of matchstick quilting. It's not difficult, but it is very time-consuming. Matchstick quilting is quilting lines around ⅛" (3 mm) apart or less all the way across your quilt.

I start by quilting my usual lines, using the edge of my walking foot as the guide. On my machine, these lines are just less than ½" (1.3 cm) apart. As I make these lines, I can remove all my basting pins. Then I go back across the quilt top and stitch down the center of each space. Finally, I stitch between those lines, avoiding stitching down seam lines as I go. If there happens to be a seam line where I should be stitching a line, I just stitch to one side of it. I know that all my lines are not going to be exactly straight, and I am okay with it.

That's a lot of time spent at the sewing machine, but it looks great when it's done. I sometimes use a pale variegated thread, shades of gray, or maybe pastels to add extra depth to the design. I'll also add random lines of different colors or weight of thread or leave some spaces unstitched for extra interest. You might think that the quilt would be stiff, but it softens after washing and stays really flat.

Grids and Plaids

How about some grids? Grids are just straight lines crossing over each other. I like grids with spacing

A simple block with matchstick quilting. This took 90 minutes to complete.

TIP

If you are having problems with drag or little tucks when you cross over a line on the larger grids, try adjusting your walking-foot pressure. Also remember to think ahead, so you can spread any extra fabric out between lines as you stitch at a consistent speed across your quilt. Use your hands like a hoop as you stitch, and you'll have a beautifully flat quilt.

that is related to the pieced design in some way, using direction and spacing.

A small-scale grid works much the same way as matchstick quilting, unifying your design and adding a wonderful texture to your quilt.

On a larger grid, double lines add so much more form than single lines. Sometimes I'll use a combination of threads to give a plaid effect across the quilt. Use a heavyweight thread in a contrasting color so you can really see your stitching. It's a great look when you want a more masculine finish.

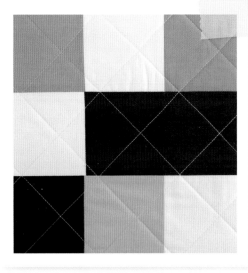

An evenly offset diagonal grid makes a pleasing allover design. By offsetting the lines from the corners of the blocks, you have built in a margin for lines that are not completely straight!

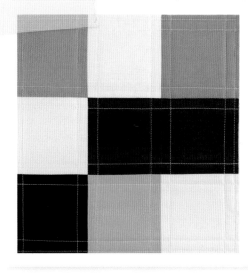

A square grid at a greater distance from your seam lines is more visible. Try a bolder thread color for a strong design line.

Plaid designs are fun to do. Experiment with different numbers of lines and spacings.

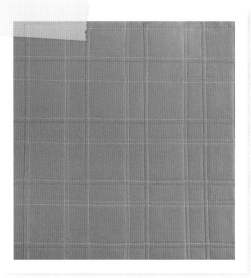

Using different thread weights adds interest to a plaid design.

BEYOND STRAIGHT LINES

Plain straight lines will look super on your quilts, but sometimes you'll want more. Here are some ideas for adding lots of extra interest and design to your stitching.

Organic Curves

Once you have straight lines down, try some gentle curved lines. You can use a chalk marker to draw your first line if you prefer. Place your hands in their usual position on either side of your stitching and slowly guide your quilt sandwich through your machine following the chalked line. Don't worry if you don't follow the markings exactly. It's better to keep the line smooth and brush the chalk off later. Use the edge of your foot for the next line, looking at the point on the foot right opposite the needle to keep your lines parallel. You will find that gentle curves are much easier to shadow or echo than tighter ones. Enjoy watching your design grow.

Grid

You might also like the look of overlapping curved lines of stitching across your quilt. They will add a very organic look to your finished project. Just start each line at random spacing at one edge of your quilt and gently guide the quilt sandwich through your machine, making curved lines that sometimes overlap as you go.

Branches

I also like to use organic curves for an overall branched design that completely covers my quilt top. I start by stitching an edge-to-edge first line and then going back and adding branches. Each section gets filled in individually.

1. Add branches off your original line to section your quilt.

2. Then go back and fill in each section individually for a lovely allover design.

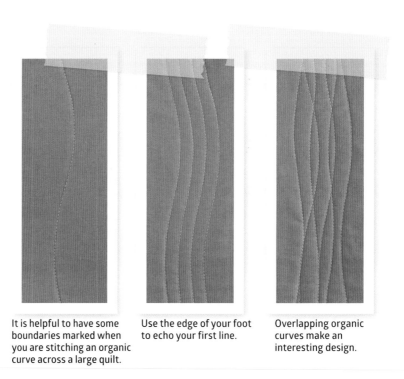

It is helpful to have some boundaries marked when you are stitching an organic curve across a large quilt.

Use the edge of your foot to echo your first line.

Overlapping organic curves make an interesting design.

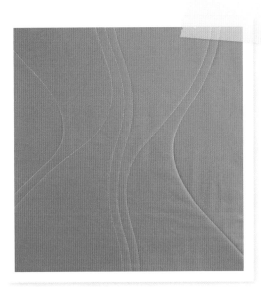

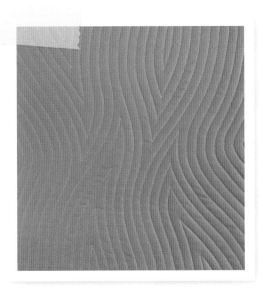

1 Add branches off your original line to section your quilt.

2 Then go back and fill in each section individually for a lovely allover design.

An organic curved grid makes an easy and quick finish for a quilt.

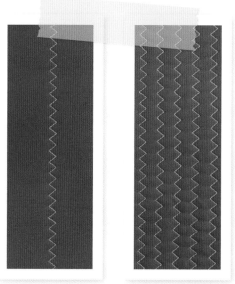

Alter your stitch length and width to make a pleasing serpentine stitch.

Rows of serpentine stitch are stitched using the edge of your walking foot as a guide.

Alter the stitch width and length of the running zigzag stitch on your machine to find a combination you like.

Stitch the rows using the edge of the walking foot for a great texture.

ALTERED STITCHES

By making small adjustments on your machine, you can alter the preprogrammed stitches on your machine to create stitches just right for quilting.

Serpentine Stitch

One of my favorite stitches to alter is known as the lingerie or running stitch (it's the number 4 stitch on my machine). It makes a multistitch zigzag line with a flat top to the points. When I adjust the width and length, it becomes a serpentine stitch. Some machines have a multistitch zigzag with sharp points that makes for a different look. Some lucky people have both stitches on their machines, and some might even have them preprogrammed, ready to quilt.

Stitching parallell lines of serpentine stitch adds a lot of texture, and it's quicker to stitch than straight lines. When washed, the resulting look is similar to an allover meander, without the learning curve of free-motion work. You can also very easilty use the serpentine stitch centered over seam lines to stabilize the seam lines.

TIP

Remember, you cannot work these stitches with a straight-stitch plate on your machine!

Stitch Number	Stitch Width	Stitch Length	Thread	Tension Change

Make note of the stitches on your machine and how you alter them, so you have them handy next time you come to sew.

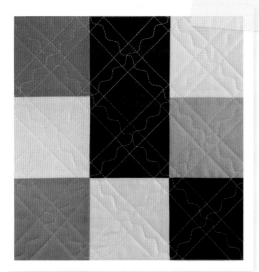

Combine straight lines and serpentine stitch for an interesting grid design.

After washing, a quilt stitched all over with the serpentine stitch will crinkle up nicely for a super cozy finish.

A simple block with serpentine stitch. This took 15 minutes to quilt.

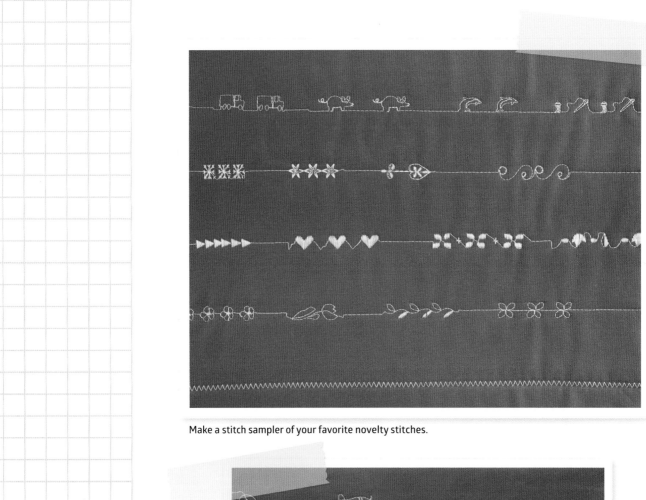

Make a stitch sampler of your favorite novelty stitches.

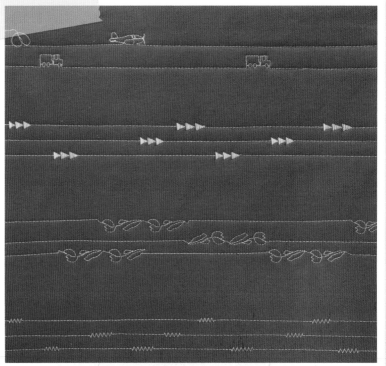

Novelty stitches included in straight lines. Note the needle position needed for a good result.

Combination Stitches

Combinations of stitches can be used to add interest to your quilting. Personally, I wouldn't want to stitch whole rows of novelty stitches across my quilts, but I like the idea of adding one or two every so often into my straight lines. Even the humble zigzag looks decorative combined with straight lines. Imagine a few stars, snowflakes, or little sailing boats!

Just start stitching with your usual straight stitch, and every so often toggle to your chosen alternative for a few stitches before returning to your straight stitch. I make my changes randomly, so that if I happen to start daydreaming and forget to change back as quickly as I intended, it doesn't matter too much.

You will probably need to adjust your needle position for the straight portion of your work to have a nice result with some of the novelty stitches. Some novelty stitches start in a position other than the center, and you need to make sure you don't have a big sideways jump in your work. Be sure to try your ideas out on a trial sandwich before you start sewing on your precious quilt top!

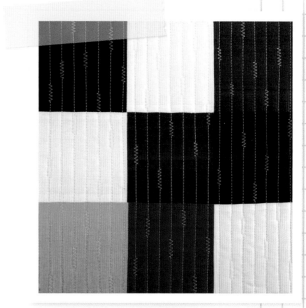

Combined zigzag and straight lines make a simple but interesting design.

Stitch Number	Stitch Width	Stitch Length	Needle Position for Straight Stitching

Remember to make notes for future reference.

SPECIAL DETAILS

I usually try to finish my quilts with edge-to-edge stitching, but sometimes I want to do something more special. These next designs require turning your quilt as you stitch.

Filling In Multisided Shapes

I love the look of a spiral of straight lines filling in straight-sided shapes on my quilt tops. These spirals add so much texture and dimension. The first quilt that I completed in this way was my Long Winter quilt. I had made lots of little log cabins and put them together, and now I wanted to quilt inside every log. I started from the outside edge of each block and worked inward. I realized that sometimes I was getting a really good sharp corner, and sometimes my stitch was jumping across the corner. I worked out that if I made an extra stitch in place at each corner—something I was doing by accident if I didn't take my foot off the pedal quick enough—I got the sharp corner I was looking for. That extra stitch locks your stitching tight. So now I deliberately stop and make that extra stitch, and I get great results.

There are two easy ways of completing a locking stitch on corners. If the button to drop your feed dogs is easily accessible, simply stitch to the corner and stop with your needle down. Pivot your quilt to make sure you are in the right place and then drop your feed dogs and take one stitch. Your quilt will not move! Bring the feed dogs back into use and start sewing again, enjoying the look of your sharp corner. If you cannot get to your feed-dog button while you have a quilt on your machine, then you will need to stop at the corner, pivot, carefully take an extra stitch while you hold tightly onto the quilt to stop it from moving, and start in the new direction.

The log cabin blocks have 90-degree corners, so it's relatively easy to use the markings on my machine foot to know where I should stop and turn. If I am filling in oddly shaped and irregular spaces, it's a little bit more difficult. I get around that by marking the center of each point with a chalk line and making that my turning point. It's worth the extra step!

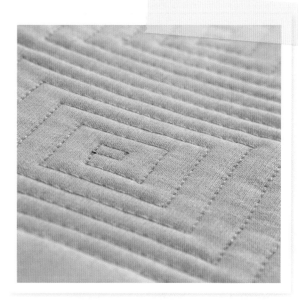

Straight-line spirals add amazing dimension to your quilt.

> ### TIP
>
> Many quilters have found that they can successfully finish their quilts once they add the walking foot to their machine and practice a little. Start out with a smaller project, such as the placemats included in the project section of this book. It's more enjoyable to work on something real rather than using a practice quilt sandwich of random fabric and batting. The seam lines in an actual piece make for a much better experience.

Straight-Line Spiral

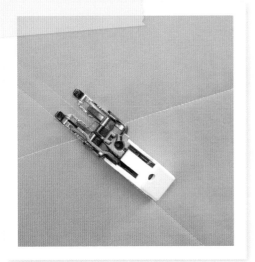

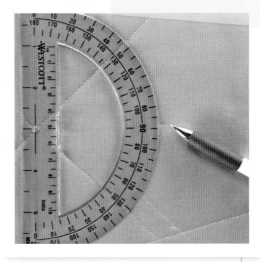

1 Before you start stitching a straight-line spiral, you should divide the angles to find your pivot points. Begin by drawing in your first stitching line with a chalk pencil. Use your sewing machine foot as a guide if you need to.

2 Use a protractor to divide the next corner you come to.

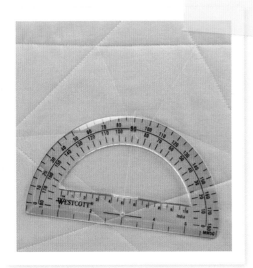

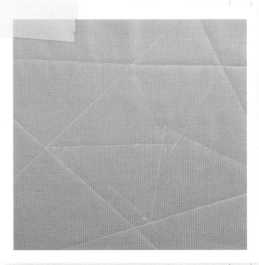

3 Work your way around all the corners. The dividing lines will be your pivot points.

4 The last corner should be measured from your initial stitching starting point. The lines will not meet in the middle!

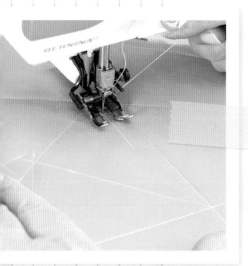

5 Start stitching at the edge by the first corner, pulling up your bottom thread and taking five small stitches to secure your work.

6 When you get to the next corner, pivot at the drawn line.

7 Check that you are in the right place by looking at the edge of your sewing machine foot. Take a stitch in place and then continue in the new direction.

8 Carefully continue stitching and pivoting.

9 Work your way into the center. Finish with five small stitches.

10 Completed straight-line spiral inside multisided shape.

Spirals

Spirals make a super addition to many of my quilts. They add an extra line of design and sometimes provide a focal point where one was missing. I usually use them as an embellishment to an otherwise quilted quilt, and I'll even change to a heavyweight thread (changing my needle and adjusting the tension as necessary) to make them stand out more. If you are working on a quilted piece, you can switch your foot for better visibility. I use my open-toed appliqué foot for good results.

I know some people like to use a spiral as the only quilting on their quilts. I have found that it is difficult to avoid distortion, however, especially in the corners. Reducing the presser-foot pressure and taking extra care will help, but I have the best success when I stitch at least some grid work first for stability. If you use a fine thread for the grid, it will fade into the background, and you can switch to a bolder thread for the spiral. And your quilt will remain square!

Stitching a Circular Spiral

I start each spiral in the center and work out. I start by pulling up the thread from the back and slowly taking one stitch at a time, rotating the quilt around 45 to 60 degrees between each stitch. With practice, you will work out how far to move the quilt, and your spirals will become more even. After the first rotation, take two stitches each time. Once you have stitched a few rounds, you can use the edge of your foot as a guide and increase your speed, stitching until your spiral is as big as you want it to be.

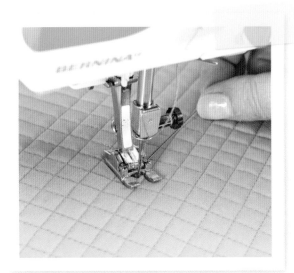

1 Bring your bottom thread up to the top.

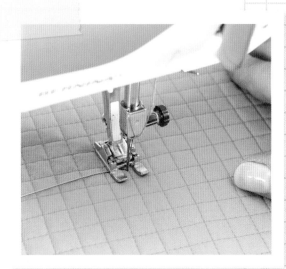

2 Holding both threads in your left hand . . .

3 . . . take one stitch at a time, rotating your quilt about 45 to 60 degrees between each stitch.

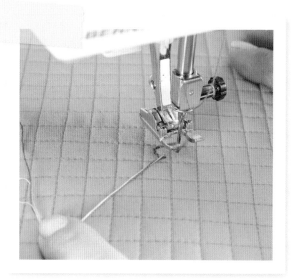

4 Remember to lift the presser foot each time you rotate the quilt.

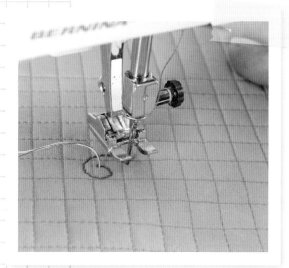

5 The spiral will gradually grow out from the center . . .

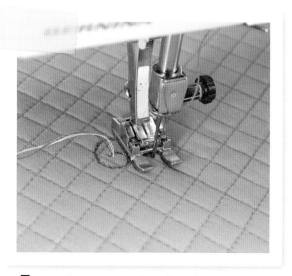

6 . . . until you can use the edge of your foot against the previous stitching.

7 Keep sewing carefully and evenly until your spiral is the size you want.

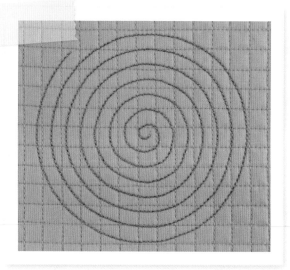

8 Completed spiral.

BURYING THREAD ENDS IN A SPIRAL

When I use a heavyweight thread (e.g., #12 weight, which is the heaviest you can put through the top of most machines), I need to bury my threads at the beginning and end of each spiral. I use a self-threading needle to make this easier. Thread the needle with both threads and take the threads to the back of the quilt. Make a very small backstitch at the end of your stitching and then take a long stitch into the batting, coming out at least 1" (2.5 cm) away and taking care not to come out on top at all. Wiggle the needle a little as you go through the batting to anchor the thread. Then pull gently on the emerging thread and cut closely. The end will disappear into the layers and be held securely.

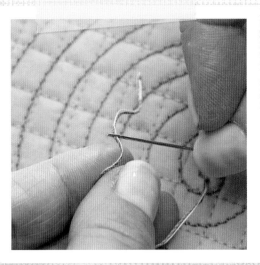

1 Use a self-threading needle to take the threads through to the back of your quilt.

2 Push the threaded needle carefully through the layers.

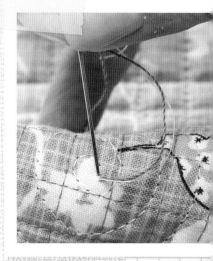

3 Take a tiny backstitch to act as a securing knot . . .

4 . . . and guide the needle through the batting. Avoid piercing the front of your work, coming out instead about 1" (2.5 cm) away from the backstitch knot.

5 Trim the threads.

CHAPTER 3

Free-Motion Quilting

I love my walking foot and all the ways I can use it to finish my quilts, but sometimes I'm looking for something a little more curvy, loopy, or unexpected. I change to a free-motion foot, put my feed dogs down, and off I go on a new adventure!

MACHINE SETUP BASICS

All the basics of preparation and basting also hold true for free-motion quilting. Your quilt sandwich needs to be flat and secure before you start stitching, and machine setup is the same with one marked difference: You need to change the foot and lower your feed dogs. Check your owner's manual to find out how to lower the feed dogs on your machine. Some machines require you to cover them, while some have a lever or a button to press.

Visit your sewing machine dealer to look at all the options that are available for you to use.

My favorite free-motion foot is one that is open-toed and offset for maximum visibility.

Free-Motion Feet for Your Sewing Machine

There are several choices of free-motion machine feet available. A visit to your sewing machine dealer will show you what is offered for your machine. This foot might be described as a darning or embroidery foot. Most have a spring as part of the attachment that lets the foot hop up and down as you stitch. Make sure you know how to attach it securely to your machine so that it works properly and doesn't fall off when you are in the middle of your design.

I like a foot that gives maximum visibility when I am sewing, so I choose a metal horseshoe shape for most projects. The foot part is offset so I can see behind it quite well, and it's open at the front to see where I'm going. It's also wide enough if I want to use a small zigzag stitch in my design.

The one problem with the open foot is that the toes can catch if I am quilting an embellished piece. In that case, I would switch to a closed foot. The visibility is not quite so good, and I can only use a straight stitch, but this is more than made up for with the toes not catching in my embroidery. I have also used a closed foot to quilt a painted piece, where the paint was making it more difficult to stitch. A closed foot holds the sandwich more firmly, lessening the tendency for skipped stitches.

An alternative is a clear plastic foot. This foot has a wide opening and is closed, so it's not going to catch. I find the glare a little distracting, but some people like this foot the best.

If you are using a high-loft batt, then a larger foot will help your machine make more even stitches and avoid puckering. A foot with a large plastic surround keeps the area you are stitching flat. There are often markings on the foot for shadow stitching, which you might also find helpful.

Find the foot or feet that work best for you and the type of quilts you are making.

Straight-Stitch Plate

Virtually all free-motion quilting is done with the needle going straight up and down. Once again, adding the straight-stitch plate to your machine will make a huge difference to the quality of your stitches. Occasionally, you may choose to free-motion quilt with a zigzag stitch, in which case you will need to switch back to your universal plate.

Bonus Tools for Free-Motion Quilting

There are many gadgets and tools available, all specially designed to help the free-motion quilter. I enjoy stitching with a great sewing machine, set into a cabinet with my favorite feet, thread, and needles. I don't use any particular gadgets, but that doesn't mean you can't!

I know that some quilters find a pair of gloves helpful. There are specialty gloves available with rubber grips on the fingertips and palms, made to make it easier to guide your quilt through the machine. A silicon sheet placed under your quilt on the machine bed might help your quilt slide more smoothly.

Various hoops and holders that go on top of the quilt sandwich can help if you have issues with arthritis or soreness in your hands. Some quilters find guiding a hoop adds less stress to their joints than holding on to the quilt itself.

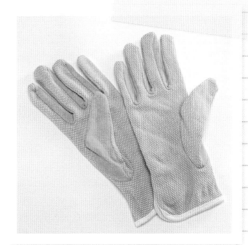

Some people find a pair of quilting gloves helps them handle their quilts with less strain.

My advice is to try the tools available and see if they help you. Find a shop that will let you try before you buy if possible. Some tools are quite an investment, and you want to make sure that what you are buying will be useful.

Another great way to try out quilting gadgets is to ask your quilting friends to a gadget party. Have everyone bring all the machine-quilting gadgets they have ever bought, and everyone can try them out. You might find that what hasn't worked for one person is just what someone else is looking for! Trading terms will be up to you to decide.

FEAR NOT FREE-MOTION QUILTING

A new adventure like free-motion quilting can be daunting, but I like to remind quilters that it's similar to learning to drive.

In England, you can get a driver's permit and start learning to drive at age seventeen. My parents booked driving lessons for me as a seventeenth birthday gift, and the instructor showed up at our house in her dual-controlled car. After a brief introduction to the three pedals in the stick-shift car and the various levers and knobs, we made a shuddering start, and I was on my way.

I took a lot of lessons, practiced with my dad, and managed to pass my driving test on the first try. I was considered safe to drive but not much better than that. A series of events meant that I didn't get many chances to drive for the next few years.

It was eleven years before I had a car of my own to drive whenever I wanted. At first I was still like a beginner—and it was exhausting! But after a few years I was able to drive long distances, find my way around strange cities, and even enjoy the journey.

Around 90 percent of the adult U.S. population has a driver's license. That's a lot of people who have learned to do something that's potentially very dangerous and difficult! Yet I meet a lot of budding free-motion quilters who have tried and given up because they didn't get good results the first time they tried. It's my hypothesis that given both a strong desire and a lot of practice, free-motion quilting skills can be learned and enjoyed by at least 90 percent of all quilters!

BEGINNING FREE-MOTION STITCHING: LET'S GO!

The most uncomplicated design to make with the walking foot is a straight line. With walking-foot quilting, the combination of feed dogs and walking foot moves your work through the machine for you and produces beautiful, controlled, even stitching across your quilt top. But now, with the free-motion foot on your machine and the feed dogs lowered, it's up to you to manually move your sandwich through the machine! When you put your foot on the pedal, the needle will start going up and down. The length and direction of your stitch is completely up to you.

I like to practice all my designs with a doodle first. The same type of learned muscle-memory that helped you learn how to write, ride a bicycle, or play a musical instrument is going to make it possible to make beautiful smooth-stitched shapes. As you doodle and then stitch, you will build up

pathways in your brain that will guide you at the machine. Even though it's the pen that moves when you doodle and the fabric you move when you stitch, doodles do help your stitching. With practice, you really will be able to relax and trust your instinct.

Wavy Lines

The easiest way to start your free-motion journey is with a wavy line. Use a fine marker and drawing paper to make some curved lines. Try going up and down the page. Note that if you stop in one place, you will get a blot of ink. It's more helpful to make smooth lines than beautiful evenly sized curves. As you begin to get used to letting the line flow, draw some lines from side to side.

Now, try it out at the sewing machine. Practice on a small basted piece to begin with, until you get comfortable with the combination of machine speed and moving the quilt top. Take a few safety pins out in the area where you are planning on stitching.

Bring your bottom thread up to the top and hold it along with the top thread in your left hand. I hold my hands in a hoop shape around the needle, gently keeping the fabric flat and ever so slightly taut. It sounds more complicated than it is!

Make four or five small stitches to anchor your thread by moving your quilt ever so slightly while you press lightly on the pedal. Finish each time with the needle in the down position. Once your threads are anchored, you can trim them and start the wavy lines.

Wavy Lines

TIP

To practice doodling, you can use the doodles in this book. Simply photocopy the doodle you want to try, enlarged to 200% percent, and trace over the lines.

Move the quilt away from you as you start stitching. Listen to the motor and observe how fast the needle goes up and down. I aim for an even medium-sized stitch with my machine running at an even medium speed. If you run the machine fast, you need to move your quilt quickly. Learn to work at the pace that is best for you.

Stitch your first line and then reverse direction by simply moving the quilt toward you. Use the edge of the foot to help space your lines. You do not need to turn your quilt around! This, of course, is the joy of free-motion stitching. You can work in any direction you choose. If you find your hands slow down just before you change direction, then you will need to release the pedal and slow your machine. Otherwise, you will get a blob of thread at the point, just like the ink blot when you doodled and held the pen down too long in one spot.

When you get close to a pin, you need to stop and take it out. Be sure to stop with the needle down. This is a great time to move your hands and re-form your "stitching hoop." Check the tension on the back of your work and make any adjustments necessary. Remember the rules from walking-foot quilting.

Keep stitching your up-and-down wavy lines until you feel ready to go side to side. This is a little trickier. You probably haven't tried stitching left to right before! Some machines take to this movement better than others. If your machine suddenly loses its tension control, try slowing down to allow the mechanism to finish each stitch completely in the less-than-ideal conditions of stitching side to side.

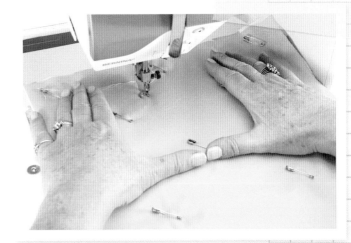

Begin by using your hands as a hoop, keeping them behind the safety pins.

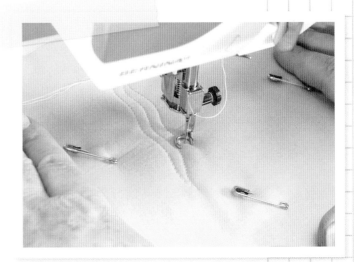

Move the quilt sandwich smoothly as you stitch.

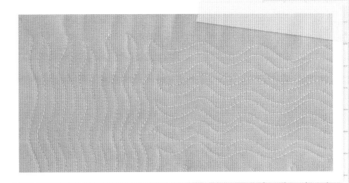

Start your free-motion adventure with wavy lines.

Your Name

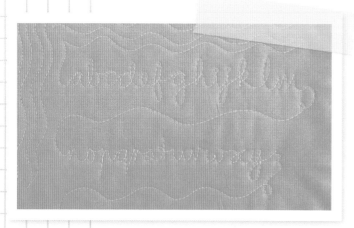
Stitch alphabet letters.

Writing

After wavy lines, the next easiest thing to try is writing your name. You already have the learned muscle memory for writing. You might need to alter the letter formation just a little to make a completely continuous line. If it feels too complicated, you have my permission to not dot your i's and cross your t's, at least to begin with!

After you've stitched your name, try lines of e's or l's. One of my favorite lessons in elementary school was handwriting, where we did pages of script just practicing a few letters at a time. Channel your inner child and quilt some pieces with your favorite words.

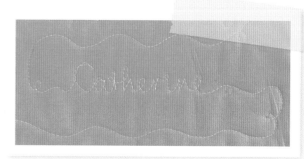
Write your name.

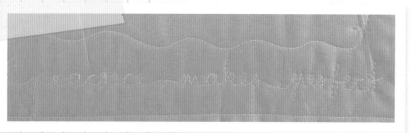
Try a phrase!

THE DIFFERENCE BETWEEN A STIPPLE AND A MEANDER

A stipple has lines that are up to ¼" (6 mm) apart. Anything bigger than that is described as a meander. You probably have used a large meander if you have ever used the stipple motif as an allover design for a quilt!

BASIC ROUTE MAPS

I think of my quilting designs as maps where I have worked out the route I need to take before setting off. This takes one of the unknowns out of the process, giving me brain space to concentrate on keeping my stitches even as I maneuver my quilt under the needle.

Stipples

When quilters think of free-motion quilting, stippling is often the first thing that comes to mind; it's frequently used as the default allover free-motion stitch. I'm not sure why that is, as in my mind the stipple stitch is a difficult one to master. That being said, let's have a look at it and work out how to add it to your design vocabulary.

Stippling is usually described as a continuous line that doesn't cross over itself and is less than ¼" apart. When you envision the stipple as an echo or shadow, then you will be able to avoid loops and crossovers.

Master quilter Diane Gaudynski taught the most understandable way to form the stipple stitch that I have ever heard. She sees it as an echo stitch with the addition of mittens and cacti.

Start with a wavy line, adding in a mitten and then a cactus from time to time. Make sure to leave space between the shapes. Next, echo that line while adding in extra shapes. And keep echoing and adding shapes!

Meanders

A meander is essentially the same shape as a stipple, just bigger. I follow the same pathway, taking care to keep my stitching steady and even. It can be easy to get carried away and speed my hands up on the familiar route beyond what my machine can keep up with. This leads to longer stitches than I like. It's not a good look!

Remember, just as everyone's handwriting is different even if they have all learned the same way, you will develop your own style of stippling. Smooth and continuous is what matters. It will come with practice.

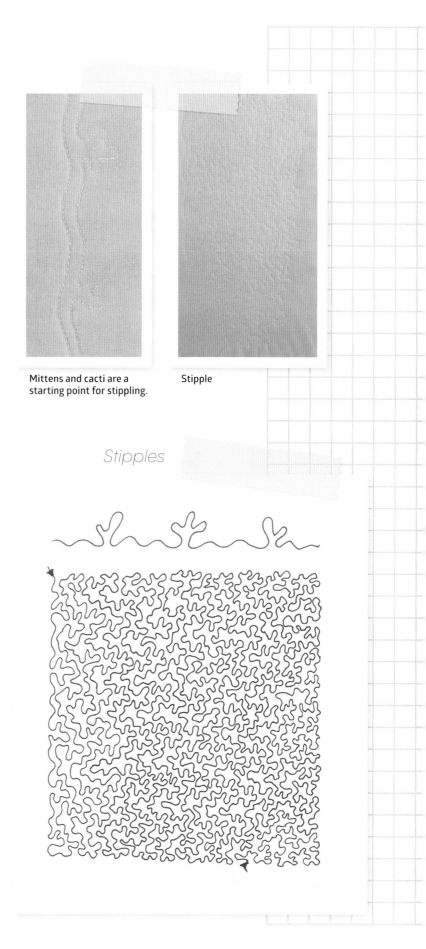

Mittens and cacti are a starting point for stippling.

Stipple

Stipples

Loopy Meander

Swirls and Loops

It was a good day when I moved on from printing to joined-up or cursive writing in my penmanship classes! However, in my English girl's school, loops were frowned upon. When my family moved to the United States, my one daughter was delighted to find that loops were positively encouraged in the cursive style.

If you have been struggling with your stippling, I think you might be happy to add some loops and swirls to your stitching. It feels more like handwriting.

Start with the doodle. As you make your line, think of e's and o's. I like to add my loops on alternate sides of my wandering line, to avoid a corkscrew look. Occasionally, two e's sit next to each other; I just don't want a whole line of them in my loopy stitch! If you find you have a bigger space between your lines than you wanted, just go back and put in an extra line. It's okay.

The only thing better than one line of loopy stitching is two lines. I often go back over my sewing and add a second line to give the look of a ribbon. You'll find this evens out your design. You can choose which side of the original line to stitch. Switching from side to side gives a lovely 3-D effect.

Adding Motifs to the Line

Once you've got your loopy-line quilting under control, you can try adding some small motifs to the design. Flowers, hearts, or stars make a good start—and as always, it's a good idea to try doodling them first.

Remember that flowers come in many shapes and sizes. Doodle until you find a shape that works for you.

I find hearts are more difficult to draw sideways. It took a lot of practice before I was happy to stitch them in any direction!

I add hanging five pointed stars on my loopy line. Vary the size and you'll be able to tuck them into any space.

Loopy meander

Double the line for a ribbon.

Quilted loopy meander with added hearts

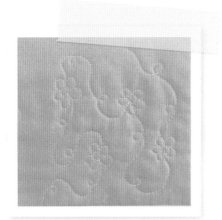

Quilted loopy meander with added flowers

Quilted loopy meander with added stars

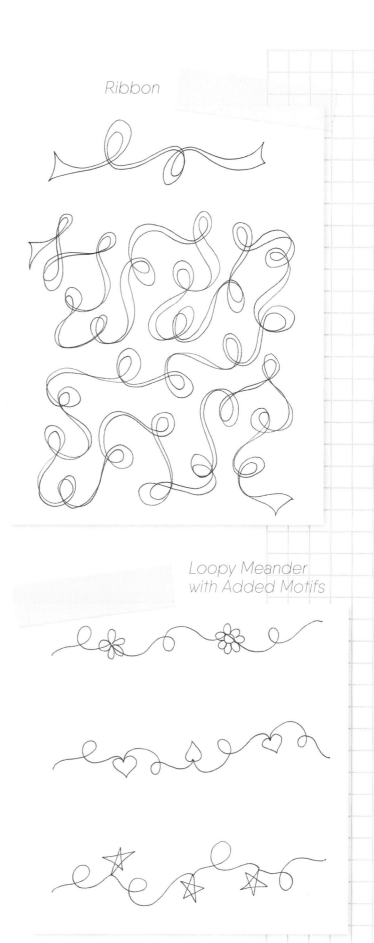

Ribbon

*Loopy Meander
with Added Motifs*

Mattress Spring (Figure Eight)

Mattress spring is what I've been calling my figure-eight design, since it sort of reminds me of mattress springs. Try rows of eights as an alternative allover design for your modern quilts. Work on keeping the two sides even as you stitch out the design and be careful to work at a consistent speed to maintain a regular stitch length around the curves. Depending on the construction of your quilt top, you may need some guidelines on your quilt to keep your lines straight. Blue tape might work for you, but if you have trouble with it coming unstuck on a large quilt, this is a time to use a grease-free chalk marker that will easily brush off your quilt top by the time you have finished stitching.

Figure eight   Figure-eight ribbon

Straight-Line Meanders

Sometimes a more angular, straight-line look is suitable for your quilt. Curves come more easily to me than straight lines, but I have practiced my angular meander. With a little care, it adds a modern look to your quilt and is a more masculine finish than the rounded loops we have tried already. Take care not to linger on the points or speed up too much on the lines. Remember to take your foot off the pedal if you stop at a corner!

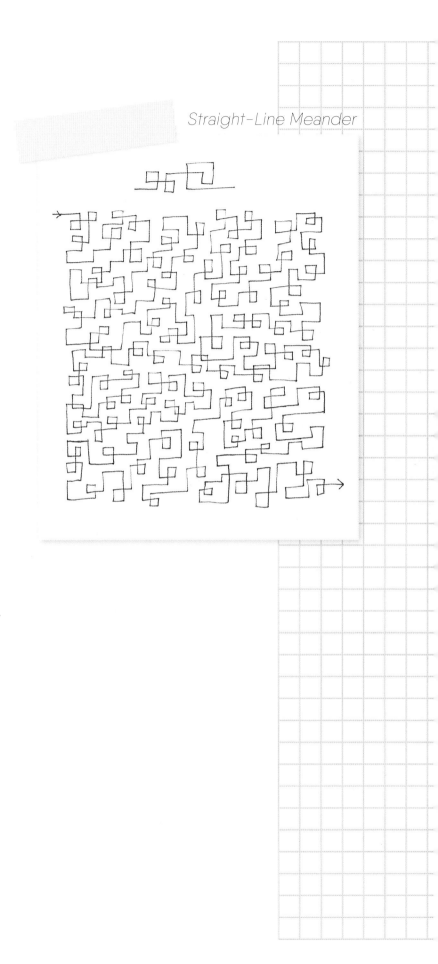

Straight-Line Meander

Straight-line meander

PRACTICING FREE-MOTION QUILTING

A good way to practice your free-motion stitching is to use a suitable printed fabric on the back of your quilts and quilt from the back, using the printed design as your route map.

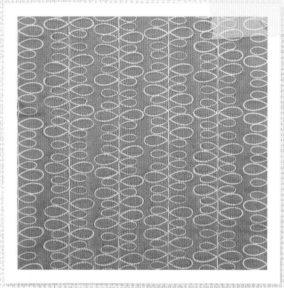

Choose a backing fabric with a simple design for some free-motion inspiration and quilt from the back.

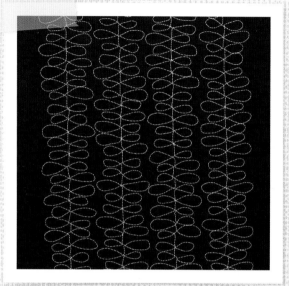

From the front

A flowered fabric also makes a good backing fabric to use to stitch from the back.

From the front

SCENIC DETOURS: UNUSUAL DESIGNS AND SHAPES

Sometimes taking the most direct route to your destination is the way to go, but I have always enjoyed time spent exploring areas off the beaten track. An allover large meander stitch is certainly functional, but not necessarily very beautiful. We have already added a few patterns to make our design line more interesting. Let's add some more!

I find it helpful to associate each design with a familiar shape. I think it makes it easier to learn how to doodle and stitch them.

Mussels

Growing up in England, I was never very far from the coast. This design reminds me of the mussels we would see clinging to the rocks at low tide. Some people think of them as garlic cloves. Start with one teardrop shape and echo it twice to give three lines before starting the next shape. Vary the size and shape of your design, and it will be easier to fill your space.

Notice how this design is drawn. The line moves up the side of the shells. If you get stuck in a corner, just take your line around the edge of your previously drawn shapes to get to where you want to be. Although I usually aim for three arcs, a fourth one will not be noticeable in the big scheme of things.

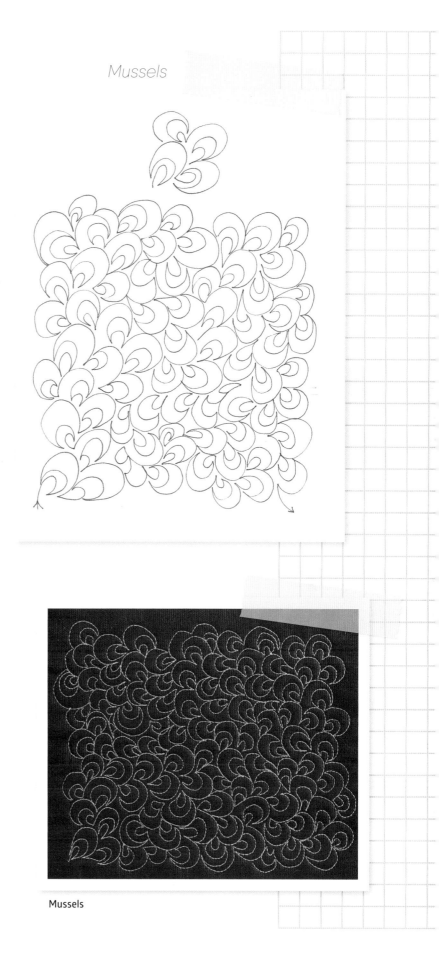

Mussels

Mussels

Flames and Waves

We go back to our very first curved line with this design. Stitched out vertically on a quilt we see flames, which provide a very active line. When the line goes back and forward horizontally, it will remind you of waves and be more peaceful.

It is usually easier to stitch this pattern with your quilt oriented to sew backward and forward toward you, rather than sewing side to side. I stitch out small areas at a time, leaving spaces in the design to blend the stitching together. Do what works for you.

Vertical wavy lines remind me of flames for an active design.

Snail Trails

I call this design snail trails because the line going in to the middle and out again reminds me of a snail's spiral shell. However, that doesn't mean that the design has to be circular. One of my variations might remind you of a tray of cinnamon buns. I find it easier to make odd shapes that fit together easily. Remember to leave space to come back out from the center! This design has a lot of potential for modification.

Snail trails

Flowers

Many of my quilts lend themselves to an allover flower design. I'm thinking of a snail shell with petals as I stitch. You can add leaves and flourishes to suit your style.

Flowers

THREAD WEIGHT DIFFERENCES

As you can see here, the weight of the thread you choose can make a big difference in the way your stitching appears.

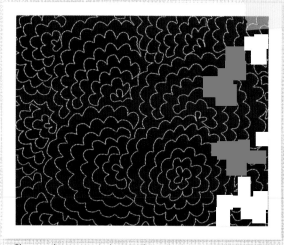

Chrysanthemum-stitch swatch worked with #50 weight three-ply thread.

Chrysanthemums

My chrysanthemum design adds a lot of texture to a quilt. Start in the center of the first flower and draw rounds of petals. Once the first flower is big enough, add buds as you go to cover the area you want to quilt. It's easy to travel to a new area of the quilt by adding more petals to a previously stitched flower.

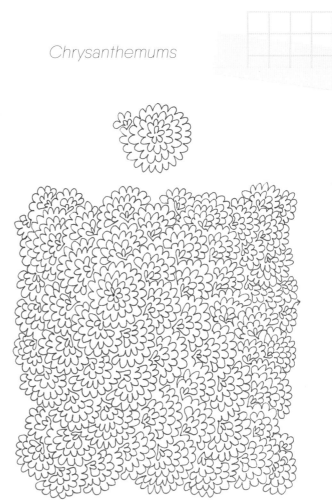

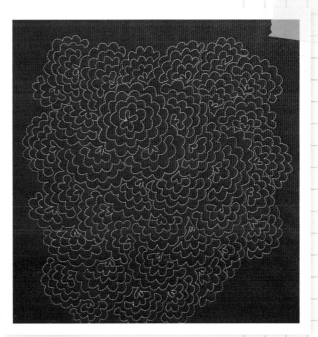

Chrysanthemums

Reverse side of chrysanthemum swatch showing texture achieved with #80 weight polyester thread.

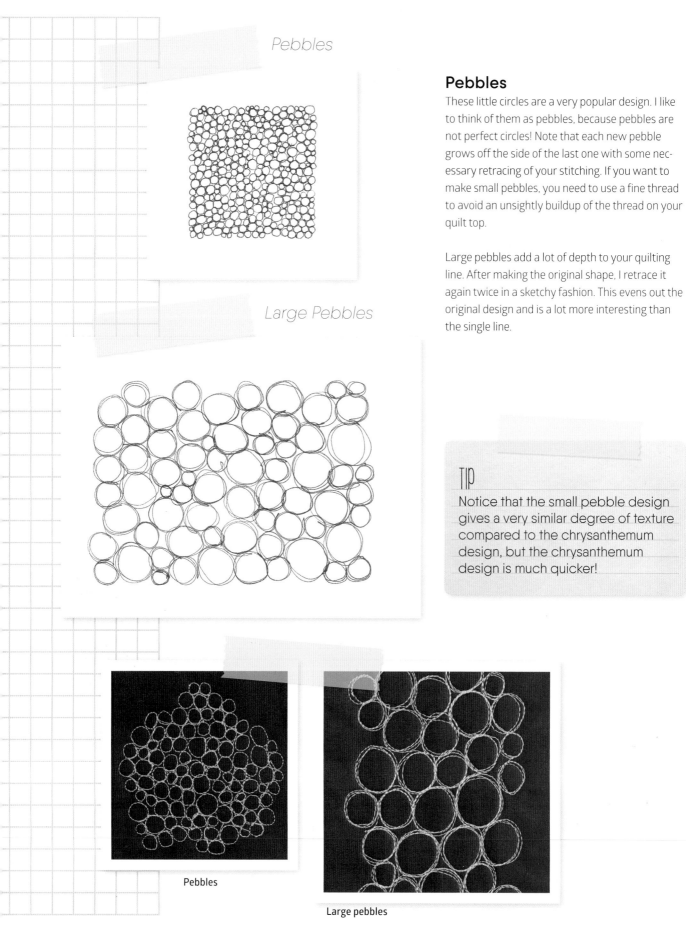

Pebbles

Large Pebbles

Pebbles

These little circles are a very popular design. I like to think of them as pebbles, because pebbles are not perfect circles! Note that each new pebble grows off the side of the last one with some necessary retracing of your stitching. If you want to make small pebbles, you need to use a fine thread to avoid an unsightly buildup of the thread on your quilt top.

Large pebbles add a lot of depth to your quilting line. After making the original shape, I retrace it again twice in a sketchy fashion. This evens out the original design and is a lot more interesting than the single line.

TIP

Notice that the small pebble design gives a very similar degree of texture compared to the chrysanthemum design, but the chrysanthemum design is much quicker!

Pebbles

Large pebbles

Puzzle Pieces

If you want to quilt a child's quilt quickly and easily, add the puzzle piece design to your stitch library! The design is worked edge to edge across your quilt top in both directions. This is one occasion when I mark my quilt top, usually with an easily removed no-grease chalk marker. Stitch a wavy line, adding an open bubble in each square. Practice making the bubble shapes on both sides of the line. You will probably find one side is easier than the other. Remember that puzzle pieces are supposed to be uneven!

E's and W's

I think of the letters E and W as I stitch this design, but sometimes an extra line creeps in. Work a block at a time to fill in the space on your quilt. You'll definitely need doodling practice if you want to avoid blobs on the many corners.

There many variations possible with this design, so make your shapes as angular or curvy as you wish, to suit the quilt you are finishing.

E's & W's

Puzzle pieces

E's and W's

OTHER DETAILS

As I began to gain confidence in my machine quilting, my repertoire of stitches grew. I realized it was easier to try something new toward the edge of a large quilt, where the bulk of the basted top would be supported at the side of the machine rather than stuffed through the small throat space to the right of the needle. I could stitch a large meander in the middle section and then add something more interesting in the borders.

As I have explored the modern aesthetic more, my quilts often don't have traditional borders. I sometimes like to designate a space for some interesting free-motion stitching before I do an allover straight-line design on the rest of the quilt.

I also like to do an allover large wavy echo or shadow line design on my quilt using a walking foot, starting the line afresh every so often. This will leave gaps as the lines converge with each other that I can fill in with one of these patterns.

Here are some designs I might use in a border or border-like situation.

Narrow Borders

I think of narrow borders as between ½" (1.3 cm) and 1" (2.5 cm). Some designs suit a small space better than others. If you like to make small shapes, then you'll love these narrow borders!

Ocean Swirl

This is a lovely swirly design. I always need to remind myself of the exact route on my practice sandwich before I start on my carefully made quilt.

Greek Key

Here is an angular version of the ocean swirl. Make sure to leave enough space to complete the design with each motif.

Vine

This adds a garden-inspired touch to a floral quilt. Try combining it with the allover flower design.

W's and E's

This is simply a single row of the W's and E's motif. Vary the exact pattern to suit your style.

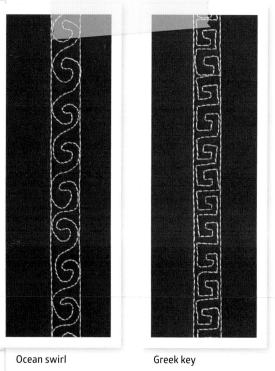

Ocean swirl   Greek key   Vine   W's and E's

Ocean Swirl   Greek Key   Vine   W's and E's

Ribbon Candy

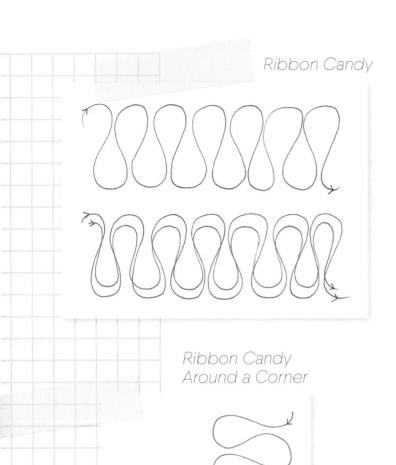

*Ribbon Candy
Around a Corner*

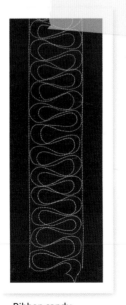

Wide Borders

Wide borders are more than 1" (2.5 cm) wide. They can be as big as you like. If you struggle with keeping your stitch length under control on large motifs as you race down your open space, try narrowing the border by making a few rows of straight-line quilting on either side of your seam lines. This will have the added bonus of defining your space and drawing extra attention to your beautiful stitching.

Ribbon Candy

The ribbon candy design is well loved by modern quilters. It is somewhat similar to the figure eights we did before but doesn't overlap at all. Doodling practice will certainly be needed to get the curves even on both sides. A second line gives depth and dimension.

If you have corners to navigate, you will find it helpful to mark them, too, if you want to keep your design somewhat symmetrical.

Ribbon candy   Ribbon candy around a corner

Mussel Variation

This design is produced when you change direction each time you start a new shell. It was one of the first border designs I mastered. If you have a good grasp of the allover mussel design, you will love using this variation in a border.

Pebbles and Lines

Everyone loves the pebble design, but it does take a long time to fill even a small area! Try this pattern instead: Stitch the circle shapes down the center of your space and then add the lines. Use your free-motion foot for the short lines so you don't need to turn your quilt as you retrace the pathway at the outer edges before making the next line. Your lines don't have to be perfect to look good, but know that they will improve with practice!

Mussels   *Pebbles and Lines*

Mussel variation as a border motif

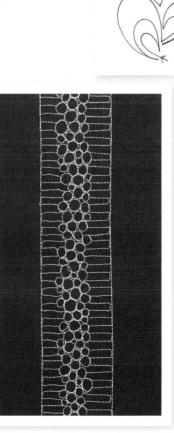

Pebbles and lines border

Feathers and Ferns

A purist doesn't necessarily consider feathers and ferns "modern," but I try not to let that concern me too much. Once mastered, feathers and ferns can add a lovely design element to many types of quilts!

Basic Feathers with a Spine

Start with this feather to get a feel for this type of quilting. There are many ways to stitch them, but my favorite style is the less formal, unmarked type. They vary every time I stitch them, and that just makes them more interesting.

Embellishing Basic Feathers

Once you have your basic feathers made, try embellishing them. The amount of embellishment you add will depend on the original size of your design and how closely you like to stitch.

An echo line around the outside of your completed feather will define it nicely before you fill in the background with one of your favorite filler stitches.

Basic feather   Feather with echo line for definition   Embellished feather

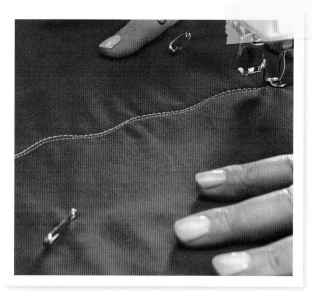

1 Start by stitching the center wavy spine and then double it by echoing back to the beginning.

2 Now add the shapes on the sides. I like to think of them as half hearts, which gives a lovely flowing line, rather than half circles. Go around the top and back down the other side.

If you find it harder to go in one direction than the other, try drawing just one side of the spine, then come back down with the half hearts.

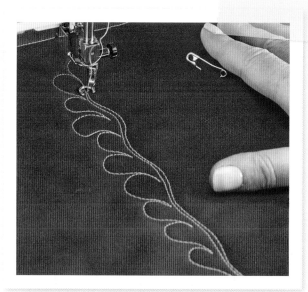

3 Now continue with the other side of the spine back to the top again, add the uppermost loop, and then stitch back down that side.

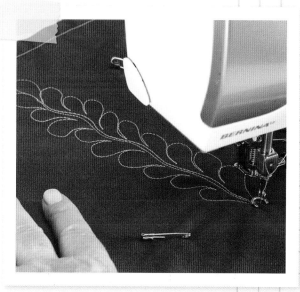

4 Having a route map will certainly help!

Spineless Feather Doubled   *Spineless Curvy Feather*

Spineless Feather

These feathers have a wonderful contemporary feel and can be used in even small spaces to add interest to your quilt top. I usually stitch them in a predefined area where I have already quilted either side of where the feather is going to go.

A chalk line is often useful to remind me where I would like the center of my design to go. I prefer an organic, curvy midpoint. Then I start at one end and stitch my feather!

Try a spineless feather with a single line or double it up for extra interest. Try using a different color or thread weight for the second line.

The absence of a spine means that there is no buildup of thread down the center of your feather. You'll get a beautiful open design. I often draw two wavy lines on a piece of paper and practice doodling in the resulting irregular space between them. Now when I start stitching, I am used to filling in all sorts of shapes, and I can concentrate on keeping my stitches even and smooth rather than worrying about where I am going.

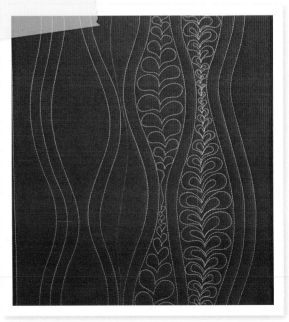

Organic curves made with the walking foot. A chalk mark provides a guideline for the center of a spineless feather that fills in the gap. Doubling the line adds further interest to the design.

Feather Borders

Feathers make a great border design. If I am making a feather with a spine, I stitch the center spine all the way around my quilt before going around again to double it. On my third pass, I stitch one side of loops and on the fourth, I complete the design—unless I want to add embellishments and fillers.

You will need to practice the corners to decide how you like to handle them. Work out a method that pleases you on paper first, so that corners don't take you by surprise when you are stitching! As long as they are neat, I don't worry about having four identical corners.

Feather as a border design

Fun with feathers!

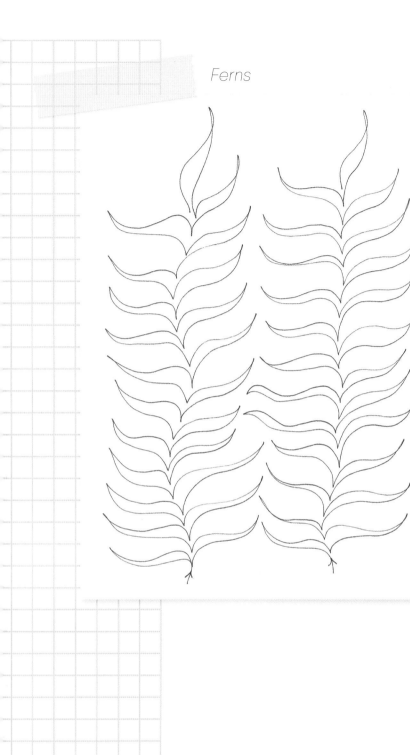

Ferns

Ferns are a pointier, more graceful variation of the spineless feather. A chalk line will definitely help you keep them stitched in your intended direction. Take care not to linger at the tips so that you don't get a buildup of thread.

The fern is a spineless-feather variation stitched on a chalk guideline.

FINDING YOUR QUILTING GROOVE

I have heard it said that practice makes perfect, but I prefer to remember that nothing has to be perfect for it to be wonderful! Practice definitely leads to improvement, and if you wish, you could ponder the rhyme we learned at school:

Good, better, best, never let it rest until your good is better, and your better, best!

—St. Jerome

I suggest that you find a couple of motifs that make sense and work for you and practice those to get used to the rhythm of your machine and work up to an even stitch length and smooth corners. Then you can gradually add to your stitch vocabulary until it becomes relatively simple to look at a design and make it your own. It really will become so much easier with practice!

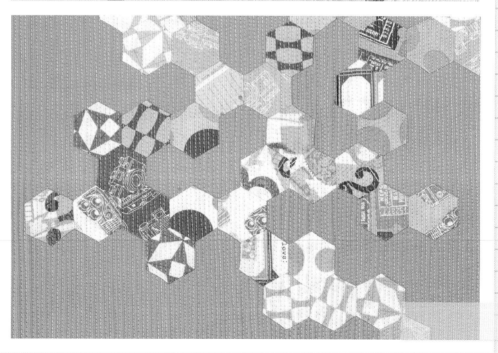

CHAPTER 4

PUTTING IT TOGETHER:

A GALLERY OF QUILTS

To give you an idea of the thought process that goes into deciding on quilting designs, what follows are real examples of quilts I have made and descriptions of the quilting involved.

As I have said before, I usually have a good idea of how I am going to quilt my quilt before I have finished piecing it. Then I know exactly how to start, and I just get on with it. However, this is not always true. In these instances, I might draw out some ideas in a small sketch format or start with some basic outlining until I have made my decision. Experience has taught me not to start until I know where I am going. It is much more difficult to take out quilting stitches than it is to put them in!

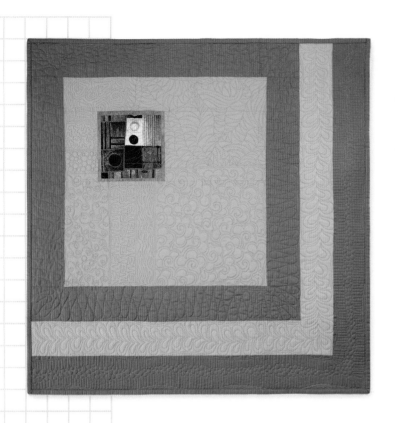

Free-Motion Sampler Wall Hanging

TECHNIQUES USED: Walking-foot organic curves with free-motion stitch sampler

I outlined the sections with organic curves made with the walking foot engaged. A different motif was stitched in each area, including the partial borders, to make a sampler of some of my favorite free-motion stitches.

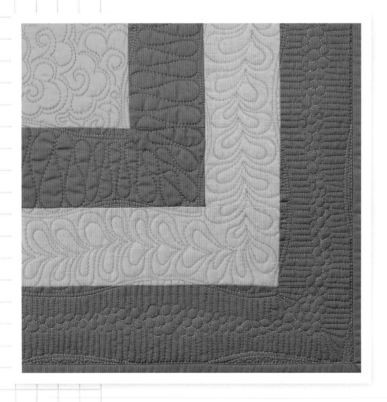

Twig Table Runner

TECHNIQUES USED: Walking-foot echo with sharp points

I stitched in the ditch around the central "twig," extending the branches out to the quilt's edges. Each section was then filled in with echoing lines, keeping the turns sharp with securing stitches made in place at the pivot points.

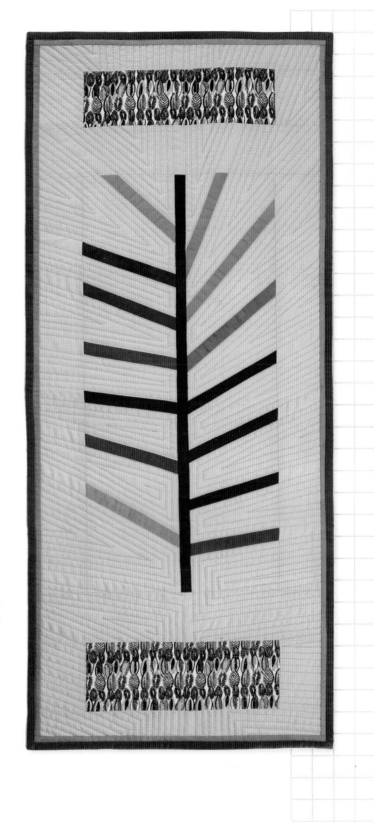

Tumbling Fun Quilt

TECHNIQUES USED: Walking-foot grid and shadow quilting with free-motion ribbon candy motif

I first stitched a grid using the walking foot over the top of the quilt, shadowing each seam line on both sides. I switched to my darning foot to work diagonally across the quilt and fill in alternate spaces with a ribbon candy–style motif. This was very good practice for changing motif size to keep a continuous line. *(pattern on page 113)*

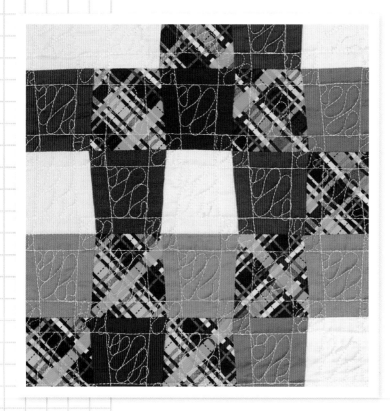

Bright Squares Quilt

TECHNIQUES USED: Walking-foot ditch stitching and diagonal grid with free-motion stippling and feathers

I stitched in the ditch to completely stabilize all the piecing in the quilt before making the diagonal grid across the center section. I used a small stipple motif to fill in each hourglass shape, taking care to work across the quilt in a way that meant I could keep a continuous line flowing and minimize my stops and starts. I finished the quilt with an embellished feather motif in the border, working around the quilt in several passes, gradually completing the design.

Keeping My Eyes above the Waves

TECHNIQUES USED: Walking-foot straight lines, serpentine stitch, and spiral

Constructed in a limited palette to represent the horizon line between ocean and sky, I knew I would quilt this little piece with serpentine stitch across the width of the piece in the lower two thirds and straight lines for the sky toward the top. I used multiple colors and weights of threads for the sea and deliberately sewed the lines closer together in some areas than others. I made a spiral in yellow #50 weight thread to symbolize the sun, but it wasn't bold enough, so I stitched a second line not quite over the top for more definition.

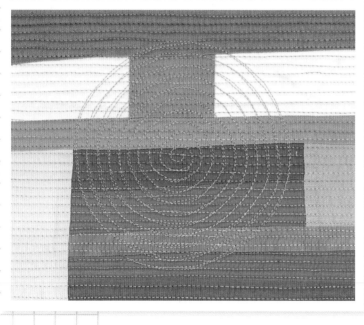

Happy Scrappy Improv!

TECHNIQUES USED: Walking-foot lines and multisided shape with hand stitching

Improv piecing always makes me happy. I stitched unifying straight lines using two different guidelines to create random overlapped areas in the quilting. The multisided shape was outlined with painter's tape and worked in from the outer edge. I added a little hand stitching with some #12 weight thread at the bottom right-hand corner.

More Than Twenty-three Hexagons

TECHNIQUES USED: Walking-foot matchstick quilting

This little hexie quilt just needed matchstick quilting right across the top to add texture. Using a #50 weight thread means that the hand-stitched design is still clearly visible!

Christmas Hexies

TECHNIQUES USED: Walking-foot grid with free-motion scribble stitching

I wanted to play with something new in the quilting of this little piece. I layered the hand-stitched piece with wool batting on top of cotton batting. I then made the straight-line grid with my walking foot, taking care with stops and starts where I met the hexagons and outlining them completely as part of this step. I then switched to my darning foot, lowered the feed dogs, and scribble stitched in alternate segments. The wool batting gives wonderful dimension to the finished quilt.

Over the Fields We Go

TECHNIQUES USED: Walking-foot organic curves with free-motion flower design

It is difficult for longarm quilters to stitch diagonals across a quilt top, but there are no such constraints on a sit-down machine. I made random groups of parallel organic curves on the diagonal across my Log Cabin quilt and then filled in the spaces in between with a flower motif. With this design, you need to be careful to avoid tucks because there is still bias stretch at play in the gaps. Think ahead and use your hands as a hoop to keep the top smooth. *(pattern on page 117)*

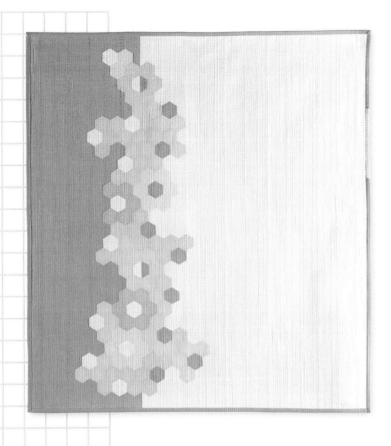

After April Showers

TECHNIQUES USED: Walking-foot irregular matchstick quilting with bold hand stitching

The hexagons were all hand pieced and appliquéd on the bicolored top. Irregular matchstick quilting with pastel #50 weight thread covers the whole design. I filled the spaces with bold hand quilting stitches using #12 weight thread in the same color.

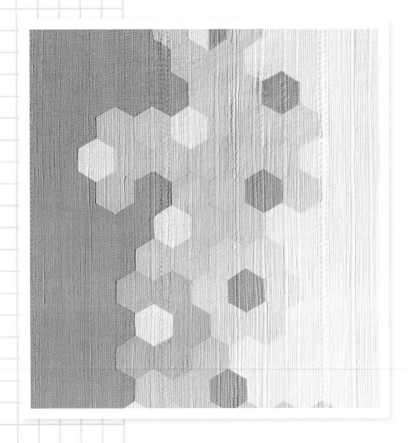

Chosen Two

TECHNIQUES USED: Walking-foot straight lines and serpentine stitch with free-motion writing

I simply used the serpentine stitch in the teal sections over the raw-edged appliqué crazy-pieced circles. I added straight lines in the mustard section, leaving spaces for free-motion script of words that mean "chosen" in some way.

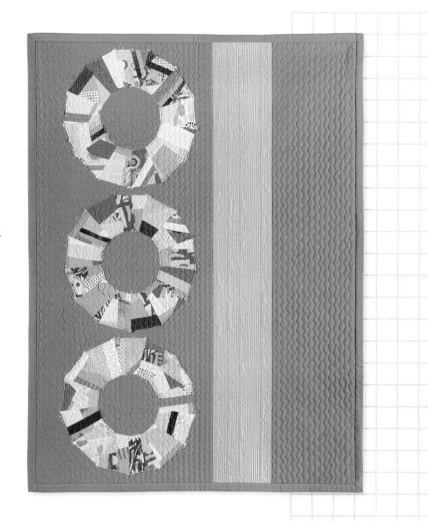

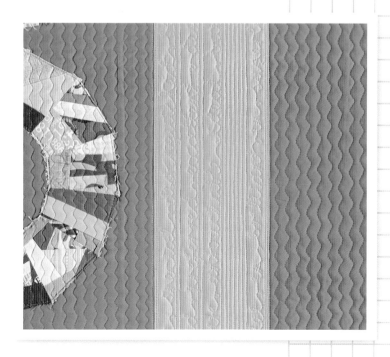

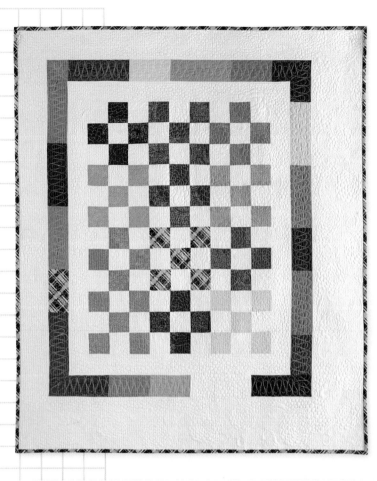

Nine Patch Brights

TECHNIQUES USED: Walking-foot organic curves with free-motion ribbon candy, chrysanthemums, loopy ribbon, and pebbles motifs

I used my walking foot to stitch a wavy line and designate a border, paying a little attention to the incomplete pieced border in the quilt top. I then switched to my free-motion foot to fill in this section with ribbon-candy quilting before covering the rest of the quilt with a mix of chrysanthemums, a loopy ribbon, and pebbles. A pastel variegated thread added extra dimension to the finished quilt.

I'll Fly Away

TECHNIQUES USED: Walking-foot organic curves with free-motion feathers and waves/flames variation

This quilt was inspired by flocks of geese flying overhead, so feathers seemed appropriate in the quilting. I started with wavy lines made with the walking foot to stabilize the quilt and delineate different sections. I then added asymmetrical feathers across the Flying Geese blocks and filled in the remaining space with a waves/flames variation, including a little extra swirl in the design from time to time.

Modern Friendship

TECHNIQUES USED: Free-motion handwriting

I ran with the modern friendship theme in this quilt. I free-motion stitched the names of all my Facebook friends in concentric squares, starting at the edge and working my way into the center. It was such fun to stitch and think about people as I added their names.

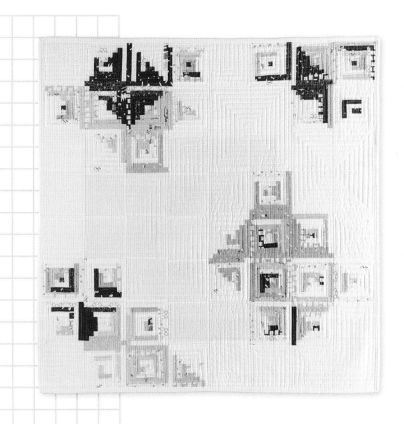

The Long Winter

TECHNIQUES USED: Walking-foot square spirals

This Log Cabin quilt was a quilt of exploration and discovery for me. It was while I was stitching the many square spirals that I discovered an extra stitch at the pivot point makes all the difference to producing a consistently sharp point. The different dimensions of the spirals add a lot of interest in the expansive negative space.

Cherrywood Squares Table Topper

TECHNIQUES USED: Walking-foot grid with spiral

I made a grid on either side of the seam lines in a blending gray thread to fade into the background. I could then put an open-toed appliqué foot on my machine to make the bold spiral in #12 weight thread, deliberately set slightly off center for maximum impact.

Cherrywood Table Runner

TECHNIQUES USED: Walking-foot organic curves and serpentine stitch with grid

Echoed organic curves across one side of my table runner contrast with a simple grid on the other half. I added a serpentine stitch on top of the curved lines for even more interest in the totally walking-foot-quilted piece.

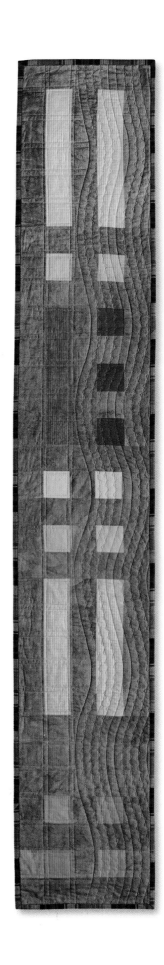

Spring in Chicago

TECHNIQUES USED: Walking-foot ditch stitching, multiple grids, matchstick, and spiral with hand stitching

This is an original design inspired by a photograph taken in downtown Chicago. I completely stabilized each section of the quilt by stitching in the ditch before I added lots of different grids on the "buildings." Dense matchstick quilting in the background helped the buildings pop. A spiral in heavyweight thread added a sun for the spring theme. A little hand stitching in the same #12 weight thread represents the people behind the windows.

Walking-Foot Sampler Table Runner

TECHNIQUES USED: Walking-foot straight lines, serpentine stitch, grid and spiral

Simple straight lines and serpentine stitching are complemented with a little grid work at one end and an off-center spiral at the other.

Small Log Cabin Quilt

TECHNIQUES USED: Walking-foot organic curves and straight lines

Fresh colors and a variety of neutrals were used in this quilt top. I quilted it with wide sections of diagonal curvy parallel lines that overlap in places, leaving gaps elsewhere. I filled in the gaps with parallel lines in the vertically opposing direction.

Clouds in the Windows

TECHNIQUES USED: Walking-foot matchstick quilting

The cloud fabric was the inspiration of this simple quilt. Matchstick quilting with gray tone-on-tone thread adds visual interest and added texture.

Winter Sky

TECHNIQUES USED: Walking-foot ditch stitching and straight-line spirals

After completely stabilizing all the "twigs" by stitching in the ditch, I filled in the sky area with straight-line spirals.

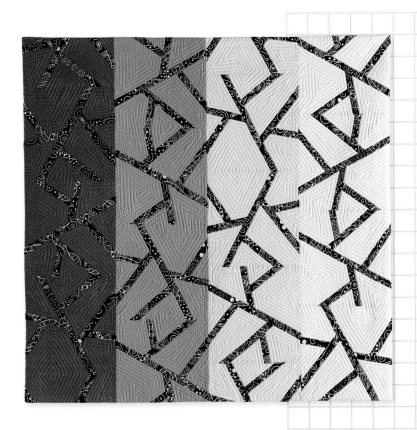

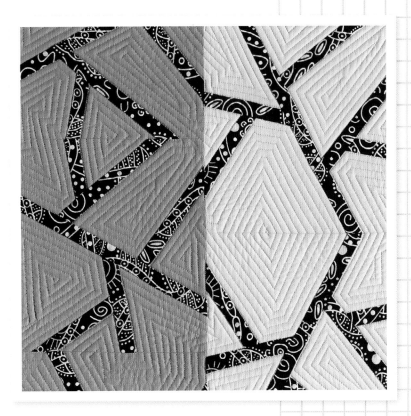

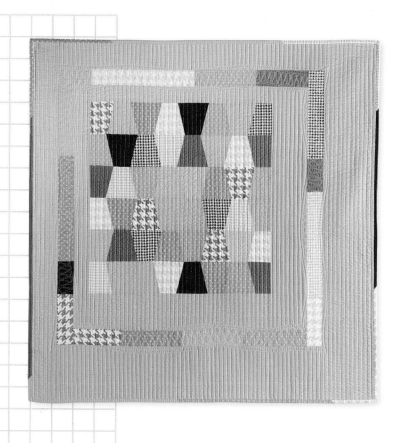

Tumbler Quilt

TECHNIQUES USED: Walking-foot organic curves and straight lines with free-motion ribbon candy

I first completed the incomplete asymmetrical border with a walking-foot wavy line and echoed it with a second line before adding the straight-line quilting. Extra care needed to be taken with all the stops and starts where the lines met the border. The quilting was finished with a little free-motion ribbon-candy stitching in the border portion.

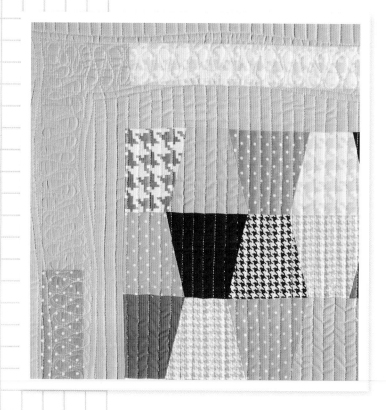

Which Way's Up?

TECHNIQUES USED: Walking-foot straight lines with free-motion fillers

This was a bigger quilt to handle and needed some planning to be successful. The walking-foot quilting came first. I started by shadow quilting the chevrons across the quilt to make sure they wouldn't move while I made the parallel lines down the quilt. The vertical seams on the quilt had been pressed open, so I shadow quilted either side of each of the seams, making neat stops and starts at each zigzag. Then I went back and filled in between them, using the edge of the walking foot as my guide. I finished off by free-motion quilting the mussel design in the cream chevrons. The colored chevrons were left unquilted for contrast.

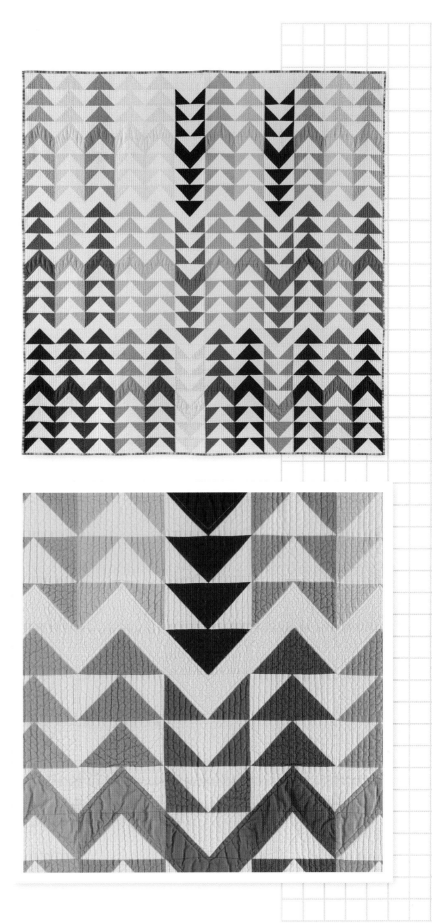

CHAPTER 5

Projects

Test out your modern machine-quilting skills on these simple yet elegant projects.

Placemats

Making a set of placemats is a great way to practice your quilting skills. Make a second set and you have a super gift for a special friend!

────────────

MATERIALS

Squares and stripe fabric: 8 fat eighths

Background fabric: ¾ yard (0.7 m)

Backing fabric: 1 yard (0.9 m)

Binding fabric: ½ yard (0.5 m)

Batting: Low-loft cotton

Finished size: 10 ½" × 14 ½" (26.5 × 37 cm) each

CUTTING

Each placemat:
From background fabric:
→ Three 10½" × 2½" (26.5 × 6.5 cm) rectangles
→ Two 2½" × 6½" (6.5 × 16.5 cm) rectangles

From chosen colors:
→ One 2½" × 10½" (6.5 × 26.5 cm) rectangle for accent strip
→ Nine 2½" (6.5 cm) squares of various colors for pieced square

From backing fabric:
→ Six 13" × 17" (33 × 43 cm) rectangles

TIP

I cut strips, 2½" (6.5 cm) wide by the width of the background fabric and then cut my pieces from these strips, trying to be as economical as possible! Cut the largest pieces first.

MAKE THE PLACEMAT
Note: All seams are ¼" (6 mm)

1. **Construct tops:** Sew nine 2½" (6.5 cm) squares together to make the pieced square. Vary the arrangement of the colors in the block; add a square of background fabric here and there for added interest. Add background strips to the top and bottom of this square, then arrange the vertical pieces as shown and stitch them together.

2. Press seams open for a super-flat finish. Match the intersections carefully. Use pins if you need them.

3. Layer the mats with batting and backing pieces. Quilt and then bind with 2¼" (5.5 cm) cut binding, folded lengthwise and sewn at ¼" (6 mm) on the front and then stitched to the back.

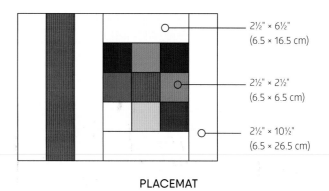

2½" × 6½"
(6.5 × 16.5 cm)

2½" × 2½"
(6.5 × 6.5 cm)

2½" × 10½"
(6.5 × 26.5 cm)

PLACEMAT

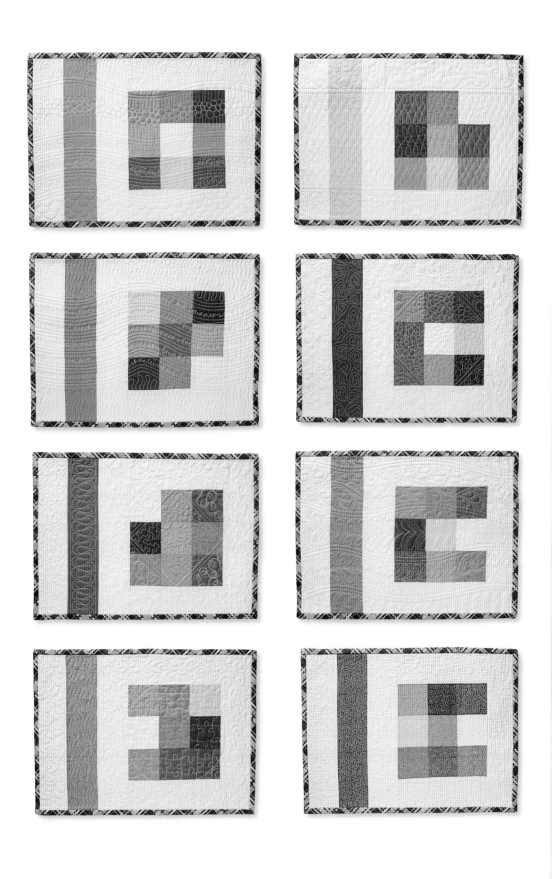

Tumbling Fun

Cut tumblers from a collection of bright solids, mix in a print, and add a neutral for a cheerful modern quilt that will make a great practice piece for your newly acquired quilting skills.

This one is shown in a small wall-hanging size. Add more or cut bigger tumblers for a larger quilt to fit your purpose.

MATERIALS

Tumbler fabrics: scraps at least 2½" (6.5 cm) square or strips 2½" (6.5 cm) wide in your choice of colors (minimum 4 strips, width of fabric)

Background fabric: ½ yard (0.5 m)

Backing fabric: ¾ yard (0.7 m)

Binding fabric: ¼ yard (0.2 m)

Batting: Low-loft cotton

Plastic for tumbler template: 2½" (6.5 cm) square

Finished Size: about 24" × 22" (61 × 56 cm)

CUTTING

Cut five 2½" (6.5 cm) strips by width of fabric from the background fabric. Subcut 4 pieces, each 24" (61 cm) long, and put them to one side for the borders. Use the leftover pieces to cut 52 tumblers.

MAKE THE TUMBLER

All seams are ¼" (6 mm).

1. Trace tumbler shape (template) onto template plastic, cut it out, and use it to cut a total of 56 colored tumbler pieces.

2. Assemble top: Arrange the pieces on a design wall. (See diagram.)

Sew the pieces into horizontal rows.

Sew the rows together.

The vertical sides will not be straight. Trim them as shown. Be sure to leave a ¼" (6 mm) seam allowance as you cut the edges of the tumblers. (See diagram.)

Measure, cut, and pin the border strips to the top and bottom.

Repeat for the sides.

3. Layer the quilt top with batting and backing. Quilt and then bind with 2¼" (5.5 cm) cut binding strips, folded lengthwise and sewn at ¼" (6 mm) on the front and then stitched to the back.

Stabilize the quilt with your walking foot and then add a ribbon candy variation for some free motion fun!

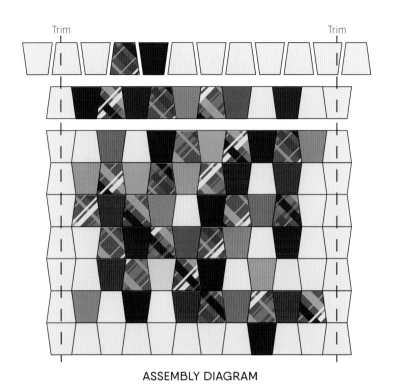

Trim   Trim

ASSEMBLY DIAGRAM

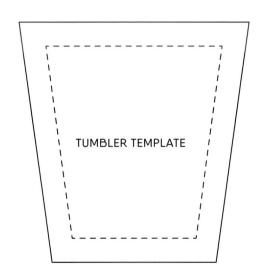

TUMBLER TEMPLATE

Over the Fields We Go

(a Log Cabin quilt)

Log Cabin blocks are very versatile. These are constructed with 2½" (6.5 cm) fabric strips. You could use jelly rolls instead of fat quarters if you prefer. It is easy to stitch more or fewer blocks to make a quilt the size you require. Alternatively, you could use narrower strips for a different look.

Once the blocks are finished, choose your favorite layout. My quilt is made with a traditional fields and furrows setting.

MATERIALS

Medium- to dark-colored fabrics:
12 fat quarters

Neutral-colored fabrics: 1 jelly roll
(you need 21–25 strips to cut all the light pieces)

Backing fabric: 3¼ yards (3 m)

Binding fabric: ½ yard (0.5 m)

Batting: Low-loft cotton

Finished Size: 54" (137 cm) square
Finished Block: 18" (45.5) square

Start with some straight line walking foot quilting and then fill in the spaces with your favorite filler designs.

NOTE

I cut my colored strips from a variety of fat quarters to create a multicolored quilt, adding a variety of neutrals from a jelly roll as my lights. If you don't wish to use a jelly roll for the neutrals, you could cut 2½" (6.5 cm) strips from yardage.

CUTTING
From each colored fabric:

→ Cut six 2½" × 22" (6.5 × 56 cm) strips. I cut extras to give myself lots of choices.

Subcut these and your neutral jelly roll strips to get a total of:

Colored fabrics	Neutrals	
9	9	2½" (6.5 cm) squares
9	9	2½" × 4½" (6.5 × 11.5 cm) rectangles
9	9	2½" × 6½" (6.5 × 16.5 cm) rectangles
9	9	2½" × 8½" (6.5 × 21.5 cm) rectangles
9	9	2½" × 10½" (6.5 × 26.5 cm) rectangles
9	9	2½" × 12½" (6.5 × 31.5 cm) rectangles
9	9	2½" × 14½" (6.5 × 37 cm) rectangles
9	9	2½" × 16½" (6.5 × 42 cm) rectangles
9	-	2½" × 18½" (6.5 × 47 cm) rectangles

MAKE THE BLOCKS
All seams are ¼" (6 mm).

1. Assemble top.

Make 9 blocks (see diagrams)

A. Stitch one 2½" (6.5 cm) colored square to one 2½" (6.5 cm) neutral square. Press toward the neutral square.

B. Stitch one 2½" × 4½" (6.5 × 11.5 cm) neutral piece to this unit. Press toward the added piece.

C. Stitch one 2½" × 4½" (6.5 × 11.5 cm) colored piece to this unit. Press toward the added piece.

D. Stitch one 2½" × 6½" (6.5 × 16.5 cm) colored piece to this unit. Press toward the added piece.

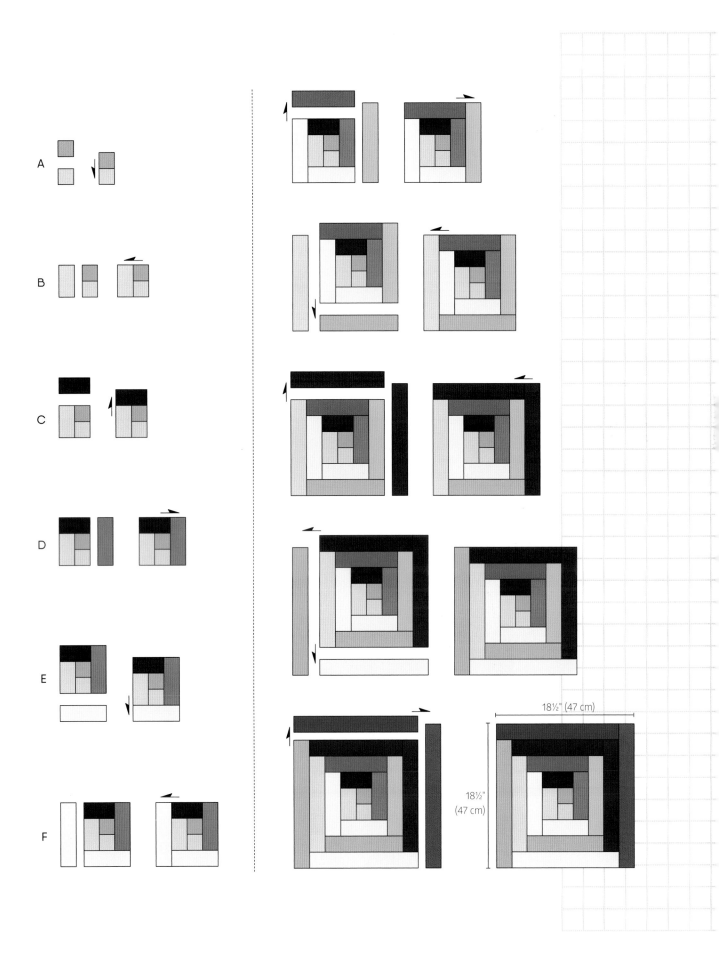

E. Stitch one 2½" × 6½" (6.5 × 16.5 cm) neutral piece to this unit. Press toward the added piece.

F. Stitch one 2½" × 8½" (6.5 × 21.5 cm) neutral piece to this unit. Press toward the added piece.

Continue adding strips in turn to complete the blocks as shown.

Lay out the blocks in your preferred setting on a design wall. (See diagram for how I arranged my blocks.)

Stitch the horizontal rows.

Stitch the rows together.

3. Layer the quilt top with batting and backing. Quilt and then bind with 2¼" (5.5 cm) cut binding strips, folded lengthwise and sewn at ¼" (6 mm) on the front and then stitched to the back.

*Special thanks to Kathleen Herbach for piecing the log cabin quilt top.

A simple log cabin quilt makes a wonderful background for some fun quilting.

BLOCK ARRANGEMENT

Which Way's Up?
(a Flying Geese quilt)

I always enjoy making flying geese units. There are many different ways to construct them.

I made positive and negative versions of each hue with the same neutral throughout for unity. The units are arranged in color groups with an interesting secondary chevron design appearing across the quilt.

MATERIALS

36 colored fabrics: 1 quarter yard or 1 fat quarter each

Neutral/white fabric: 5½ yards (5 m)

Backing fabric: 4½ yards (4.1 m)

Binding fabric: ¾ yard (0.7 m)

Batting: Low-loft cotton

Finished Size: 72" (183 cm) square
Finished Block: 3" × 6" (7.5 × 15 cm)

CUTTING
From neutral fabric:
→ Cut 14 strips, 6½" (16.5 cm) wide across the width of your fabric.

→ Subcut these strips into (146) 3½" × 6½" (9 × 16.5 cm) rectangles.

→ Cut 26 strips, 3½" (9 cm) wide across the width of fabric.

→ Subcut these strips into (288) 3½" (9 cm) squares.

From each colored fabric:
→ Cut four 3½" × 6½" (9 × 16.5 cm) rectangles.

→ Cut eight 3½" (9 cm) squares.

MAKE THE QUILT
All seams are ¼" (6 mm).

1. Assemble top.

Make 286 flying geese units. (Note that two spaces in the design are solid neutrals.)

For one unit, use one 3½" × 6½" (9 × 16.5 cm) rectangle and two 3½" (9 cm) squares. Use 2 neutral squares with a colored rectangle or 2 colored squares with a neutral rectangle.

2. Draw a diagonal line on the wrong side of the two 3½" (9 cm) squares. Place a square on top

BLOCK ARRANGEMENT

of the left-hand side of a 3½" × 6 ½" (9 × 16.5 cm) rectangle right sides together and stitch on the marked line. Trim ¼" (6 mm) outside the sewn line and press the seam toward the corner fabric.

Sew another square on the opposite end. Trim ¼" (6 mm) outside the sewn line and press toward the corner fabric again. Trim the block to 3½" × 6 ½" (9 × 16.5 cm).

Arrange the units on a design wall. (See diagram for how I arranged my units.)

Sew the vertical columns. Press the seams in alternate columns in opposite directions.

Sew the columns together, nesting the seams. Press the seams between the columns open.

3. Layer the quilt top with batting and backing. Quilt and then bind with 2¼" (5.5 cm) cut binding strips, folded lengthwise and sewn at ¼" (6 mm) on the front and then stitched to the back.

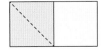 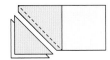 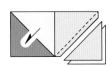 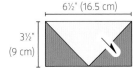

Simple shapes carefully placed makes a clean graphic design.

Index

ABOUT THE AUTHOR

Born and raised in the northwest of England, Catherine learned to knit and sew as a child. Three years after her family moved to Naperville, Illinois, in 1995, Catherine discovered quilting when she took a class at a local quilt store. And the rest is history. Today, she is a sought-after quilting teacher and speaker. Her quilts have won awards at national shows, including a first place ribbon at the inaugural QuiltCon in Austin, Texas. She is an active member of PAQA (the Professional Art Quilt Alliance) and cofounder of the Naperville Modern Quilters Guild. Catherine has appeared on *Quilting Arts TV*, is a regular contributor to *Modern Patchwork* magazine, and is the author of two *Modern Machine Quilting QATV* workshop DVDs.

Catherine and her husband still live in suburban Naperville. Her four children are all married and providing grandchildren at a good rate. Follow her quilting adventures at her website catherineredford.com.

METRIC CONVERSION CHART

To Convert	To	Multiply By
Inches	Centimeters	2.54
Centimeters	Inches	0.4
Feet	Centimeters	30.5
Centimeters	Feet	0.03
Yards	Meters	0.9
Meters	Yards	1.1

ACKNOWLEDGMENTS

Thank you to all who have made this book possible. You know who you are. I truly appreciate each and every one of you.

DEDICATION

Sheila, it's all your fault!

Discover More
MODERN QUILTING
Inspiration

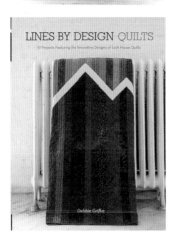